The Marriage ~~of~~ ~~~~
Spice

An Autobiography written by Dr. Kunwar Prasad Bhatnagar and Recipes of Mrs. Indu Bhatnagar.

Published by his family to cherish their distinguished lives.

Dr. Divya Cantor

Prayer to Lord Ganesh

वक्रतुण्ड महाकाय सूर्यकोटिसमप्रभ।
निर्विघ्नं कुरु मे देव सर्वकार्येषु सर्वदा॥

Vakra-Tunndda Maha-Kaaya Suurya-Kotti Samaprabha |
Nirvighnam Kuru Me Deva Sarva-Kaaryessu Sarvadaa ||

KPB Translation
O Lord Ganesh, brilliant like numerous suns,
You bless all activities by me with success.

Acknowledgments

This book is in memory of my late father, Dr. Kunwar Prasad Bhatnagar, and with love to my mother, Indu Bhatnagar. The artwork on the cover is painted by my mother in 1961 and the book cover design is created by my niece, Dr. Cami Burruss. Deep thanks for Cami's time and artistry in this humble, yet loving project. The support of Dad's colleagues, Dr. Greg Cooper and Dr. Tim Smith is tremendous in this project since his passing. I appreciate the support from my husband, David Cantor, and son, Alec Rouben, along with care from the rest of my immediate family. I am grateful for the assistance from Ms. Shruti Tiwari, a fortunate new relationship to help me bring this work to life.

In the loving memories of Dr. Kunwar Prasad Bhatnagar.

*He completed this work in parts and approached to keep it as
original as possible—a tribute to his remarkable life.*

Prologue

"I forgot my goggles, and I am missing them," said the man to me at the pool as I was completing my morning swim. It was 7:00 AM on a muggy morning at The Lalit Hotel in Central Delhi in May 2022. As I reflect on this small moment in time, "missing" now becomes a keyword. Missing an object, missing time, missing a person, or missing a loved one reflects a space that needs to be filled somehow. I miss my father. He passed away on November 17, 2021, after a long period of declining health. I was in New Delhi, India, in May 2022 to help complete the visharjan (dispersing of the body's ashes) into the holy Ganges River for my father, Dr. Kunwar Prasad Bhatnagar. I finished this journey alongside my mother, Indu Bhatnagar, sister, Jyoti Burruss, son Alec Rouben, nephew Matthew Burruss, and cousin-sister, Meeta Bhatnagar.

"Missing." Is it possible to replace goggles while in the middle of a swim? I feel like I'm in the middle of a long swim. What does one do when missing a loved one after they have passed? This project is an act of love, admittedly, a healing process for me. My father did not finish his autobiography, which remained in draft form. I have made very few edits to his entries; mostly grammatical changes and I combined some entries for proper timing and sequencing. Otherwise, his writing is as presented here and reading his words reminds me of him, every time.

My father was born in Gwalior, India, on March 21, 1934, and passed away at home, in Louisville, KY, USA, on November 17, 2021, surrounded by family and many dear friends. Dad lived a very good life; he was spiritual, always kind, always gracious, and never spoke harshly. He was a dedicated and consummate scientist, and this was his duty, his dharma in life. He began his autobiographical writing in March 2006 and recorded profusely until August 2006, with a few entries from 2014 to 2016. His last entries in May and July 2020 were relatively brief, just as the COVID-19 global pandemic hit and his health began to deteriorate.

Dad's career was remarkable in his pursuit of academic and research excellence. He published well over 150 peer-reviewed journal articles throughout his life. He continued to publish past retirement with publications continuing in the last year of his life with colleagues who remained close to him. He retired as Emeritus Professor from the University of Louisville, School of Medicine from 1972 to 2006, Associate Professor in 1978, and then Full Professor of Anatomical Sciences and Neurobiology in 1985. Dad's early education was in India at Agra University, receiving his Bachelor of Science in 1956. The Vikram University in India awarded him a Master of Science degree with honors in Zoology in 1958. Dad writes about how he was able to arrive in the United States in 1967 to complete his education under the direction of the distinguished Professor Frank Kallen at the State University of New York at Buffalo. In 1972, he earned a doctorate in anatomy. In his academic statement, Dr. Kunwar Prasad Bhatnagar proudly claimed the educational lineage of Dr. Kallen, who was a student of the acclaimed chiroptologist William Able Wimsatt (1917–1985) and, following that, the literary heritage goes back to Howard B. Adelmann (Cornell, 1898–1988), then Bert Green Wilder (Cornell, 1841–1925), and finally Louis Agassiz (Harvard, 1807-1873) a naturalist in the likes of Charles Darwin.

Dad remained a very kind mentor in all of his partnerships and relationships. Dad's dedication to service helped teach more than 5,000 medical students over 36 years at the University, and I was one of those lucky to have him teach me gross anatomy as a freshman medical student. He led by example throughout his life, demonstrating that helping others was the true goal of practicing medicine.

During the final years of my father's life, the vagaries of aging evolved. His life slowly changed, as did ours, as our family rallied to help Mom and Dad cope while ensuring they could age with grace and compassion. During the summer of 2020, with COVID-19 raging worldwide, shuttered in my home, I began another project. I followed my mom as she prepared some of our favorite dishes. I would make educated guesses as to whether the pinch of salt was ½ or ¼ teaspoon, as she does not use measuring spoons or cups. I wrote down the recipes and took a photo of each final product. This book is about their marriage of science and spice! Their marriage of 60 years revolved around Dad's scientific work that brought him and us to the USA and embedded our lives in this culture. Although Dad's work is well documented and even published, the fact is that it is my mother who raised us and took care of my sister and me. I recall our dad apologizing to me for all the extra work his ailments created. I said, "you took care of me when I was young and now it is my turn to help you." Without a moment of hesitation, he said to me, "I did not take care of you; your mother did it all." He is right in many ways. It was our mom who encouraged the pursuit of higher education for both my sister and me. From my early years to now, it is mom still shows me ways to be a better human being. It is clear how she has blossomed over the years. From my young eyes and ears, it would appear that she was a follower and did what Dad asked. As the years progressed, her determination may have been missing in her prior actions but she found the path to overt expression such that her remarkable skills shine for all to see and learn. It is our mom who secures our roots in the magical county that produced these two remarkable people. India, always.

Table of Contents

<u>Recipes</u>

Dr. Divya Cantor

My Paternal Grandparents

A sketch drawn by Dr. KP Bhatnagar in a letter written to his wife May 19, 1961.

I was born and raised in Gwalior, Madhya Pradesh, India. It was on March 21, 1934, that, I was delivered into this world as the grandchild of Munshi Gauri Sahai Bhatnagar and his wife, Shivdei, my grandmother. The time of the day was 2:15 pm, and according to the horoscope, if I were to be born an hour earlier, I would have been a world-renowned figure. My parents were Narayan Swaroop Bhatnagar (September 9, 1904 - February 21, 1966) and Bhagwati Devi Bhatnagar (June 12, 1909 - February 24, 1992). The midwife, Tasleeman Bai (Tasso Bibi), delivered me at home. I have met this gracious lady over several years, once or twice, even after returning from the United States. My mother would always make me bow down to her and offer a suitable present, which I gladly did. I only have the date when my grandfather passed away (1946). I remember the last day or two of his life when he was gradually losing his breath. It was in the two-room house we were renting from Rameshwari Dayal Saxena in Bawan Paiga, near Nai Sarak, where later my maternal uncles rented a big house from Mr. Shyam Behari Lal Srivastava. By 1946, we were many brothers and a sister. My grandfather had a particular affection for me. I remember, holding his right-hand finger, I walked with him. We took a horse-drawn buggy home in Moti Jheel, some 30 miles out of Gwalior, visiting a relative who received us with love. We were entertained lavishly. I still have the taste of the particular dessert (halwa) made from stone ground wheat.

My grandfather was one of a set of twins. His twin brother, my granduncle, was Ishwari Sahai Bhatnagar. He made Moradabad his home. My grandfather's ancestors all came from a district, Amroha, which is close to Moradabad. As a child, I remember to have visited this ancestral home, which was huge with a great courtyard, and a Shiva temple. Outside on the street, there was a tomb. This is my only recollection of our ancestral home. With my father's assistance, I have drawn a family tree on both sides and that of Indu. The latter was drawn in 1974 with Mr. BS Varma, my father-in-law. That will be made a part of this documentation. I was told that these twins were so alike that it was common to catch people confusing one with the other. I met Ishwari Sahai Babaji in Moradabad. There will be a separate section on him and his family. The twins were married in the same family, and their wives were sisters.

My grandfather, as told by my mother, was in the police department for some time. He and his force were once said to have encountered and exchanged fire with the dacoits (criminals) Dongar and Batari. A bullet was said to have passed either between my grandfather's legs or one of the dacoits. My grandfather was a scholar of Persian, Arabic, and Urdu languages. He had begun teaching me Urdu. I hardly got through the alphabet. Then, I must have lost interest in this exercise. My grandfather was the first person who took me to a formal school for admission to the first grade. That was "Gorkhi Elementary school." I was crying and did not want to enter the class. He made me sit in front of the classroom's threshold and went out to buy Jalebi (a sweet delicacy) to entice me, and he was successful. The school, that room, and that piece where I sat are still as fresh in my memory as this writing. I attended a daycare school led by a male teacher, handling 15 young children reciting alphabets or multiplication tables. That verandah still stands in the lane, Bhau Ka

Bazar, and I clearly remember the days I was in that school for several hours. My grandfather had assured the teacher that the bones of his grandson belonged to him but that the muscle belonged to the teacher, in other words, saying do not spare the rod!

My grandfather was a court scribe for a while and used to write persuasive appeals and court documents. He was an extravagant host. Every Sunday, he would invite one of our relatives, and plenty of them on both sides, his son's and his daughter-in-law's, to join us for lunch. Outside our home on Nai Sarak, where we lived in the rental homes of Shambhuji (a landlord and a businessman holding a large number of rental homes; his son was Alopi, whom I kept in touch with until 1960 or so), there was a sweet shop owned by Jaggu (Jagmohan) Halwai. On many occasions, my Babaji (grandfather) would pick up an entire dish of sweets to be used at home; and the halwai would get paid later. In his later years, Babaji opened a candy shop in a very small, closet-like space in Patankar Bazar, not far from where Pisal Tailors are now located. I remember that this shop did not run for very long. Once, I recall (as an infant), I was lying in the cradle. I even remember the hook from which the cradle was hanging by a rope. The time was in the afternoon, and the house was Shambhuji's, as mentioned above. I fully recollect my Babaji approaching my cradle and emptying his handkerchief, holding the banknotes and other coins in my cradle for me to play with. In the adjacent room, I see in my mind's eye the bedridden form of my grandmother, who was known to hide me in her overalls so that I would be saved from the onlookers' evil and harsh eyes! My mother tells me that once, while in my Babaji's lap, I suddenly got hold of the flowing beard of one of his visiting friends, pulled at it, and would not let go, causing much discomfort to the gentleman. He remarked to Babaji that his grandson was very naughty!

A photograph by my uncle (Ram Kishore Airania, husband of my mother's sister Gayadevi) shows my grandfather sitting with my edentulous grandmother lying down and my father holding me, a child of perhaps three to four years of age.

The family possessions in the room, a water container, lantern, and a cot, are also seen in this photograph. Another photo of my Babaji is from a group photograph taken in Mathura at the time of the wedding of my maternal uncle Badri Prasad Bhatnagar. He was married to Rukmani Devi (my Mami, who passed away in November 2005 at Gwalior, one of the last survivors of this generation). I remember going to the wedding party by train, the wedding at Mathura, sightseeing, and returning via a fast train. My grandfather lost the huge platter out of the speeding train while trying to clean it through the open window! I had to be a child of five or so at that time.

My grandfather was a **Shiva** devotee. He was very fond of going to Kunwar Maharaj and Kaila Maharani Temples (see the section on how I was born as a blessing from the temple) with my parents to beg for the boon of getting a child into the family. And he was blessed. These events were very well remembered by the priest of the Temple, Gulab Chand, who narrated them to me.

Babaji had a standing in the Bhatnagar community in Gwalior. At all society meetings, he led the occasion and sat with his friends, such as Gokul Kishore Bhatnagar of Bakshi-ki-Goth. For social occasions, there used to be a list of invitees, which was taken by a courier who would also distribute sweets and other gifts as desired by the families. Usually, these couriers came from the barber caste and were very useful for celebrations of all kinds.

My father and Babaji were both fonds of smoking tobacco using a water pipe (called a Hukkah). It was my duty as a child to daily clean this pipe of foul water and set up the tobacco for its early morning use. The first thing they would do is smoke while sitting together. I am so glad not to have picked up that habit. I was given a few cents (paisas) as my pocket money. I remember having used it many times. It was a better brand of sweet smoking tobacco from the shop close to the Alijah Darbar Press near Bada in Lashkar (Lashkar, Gwalior, and Morar combined formed Greater Gwalior or Gwalior). I have brought a water pipe and a clay base from my household in Gwalior. This one belongs to my grandfather.

There are hardly any articles in my possession that belonged to Babaji other than the water pipe. Another item is my horoscope, on which he wrote a few sentences in Hindi, identifying the horoscope. Surprisingly, his handwriting in Hindi is very similar to the writing in the

Vedic times in which the Hindu scriptures are written. There are a few nibs, ink-writing pens, in my possession from his era, one old cotton money belt, one call bell (ceramic and broken), one sponge case with the original sponge now stone hard. Above all, our deities which are in my home at Louisville, at Kailash's home in Gwalior, and perhaps other brothers may have one or two. No other papers are left from Babaji's time. Once at the Bawan Paiga house, I discovered a few coins sitting on the inside ledge of the stairs. I asked nobody and pocketed those. I regret it, for I always thought they may have belonged to Babaji. This happened when I was about ten years old.

He always wore heavy cotton, tailor-made jacket and also had a copper toothpick and an earwax removal pick on a black cotton chain. It is unknown to me, but I believe he was born in Almroha, Moradabad. My father seems to have been born in Gwalior.

Dr. Divya Cantor

My Parents: Mr. Narayan Swaroop and Mrs. Bhagwati Devi Bhatnagar

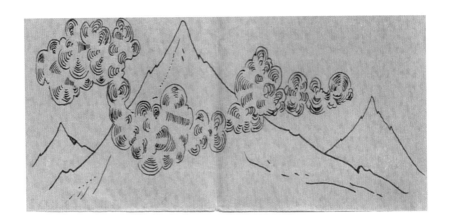

A sketch drawn by Dr. KP Bhatnagar on May 15th 1961 in a letter to his new wife.

घन घमंड नभ गरजत घोरा।

पुरथिया हीन डरपत मन मोरा॥

Ramayana

The clouds are roaring and roaring in the sky. Without Priya (Sitaji), my mind is afraid.

The Marriage of Science and Spice

My parents (we called them Pita Ji and Mata Ji) were born in Gwalior, lived their lives there, and passed away there. Pita Ji was born on September 9, 1904, and died on February 16, 1966. My mother was only about 15 years old when she married. She was the daughter of Munshi Bishan Lal Kanoongo and Baua (my Nani hailed from Banaras). They had settled at Jora Alapur, a village on the Gwalior-Shivpur railway line, some 40 miles from Gwalior. They belonged to the respectable families of the village and lived in a small castle-like home, of which I have perfect memories of the layout. I, as a child, visited that home with my mother several times, one of these being when my maternal uncle, Badri Prasad Bhatnagar, was married in Mathura. The bridal party left from Jora-Alapur.

My only remembrance of my Nana Ji was of him dressed in a Sherwani-Chudidar Pajama, ready to set out with the marriage party, or may have been even an earlier occasion. I would not be more than five years old, but I have a permanent impression of that sight. My Nani lived for several decades after Nana Ji passed away. She moved with both her sons to live at the Bawan-Paiga house of Shyam Behari Lal. I was very fond of visiting her and would always sit with her. She would bless me, ask how my mother (her daughter) was, and give me a laddu from the metal box kept near her pillow. One day, we learned the sad fact of life that she had passed away in the morning. It was in this house that the entire household (all members) of their four daughters, around 10 to 12 people in each family, would get together with the families of her two sons. (My Bade and Chote Mamaji), easily fifty or more people, several times a year, at major festivals for celebration and dinner. Both my mama Jis were the most generous, scholarly, and respectable people who ever lived. I will return later to the time I have spent in the learned company of my Mama Jis.

Pita Ji was a devout Hindu. He was a great follower of the Kunwar Baba and Kaila Maharani Temples. He told me the following incidents, later confirmed by my mother. Their first child was a daughter who did not survive infancy. Devastated, the parents waited for another child, but none came for years and years. They were directed to the Temple, as mentioned above, where they began to go religiously every Monday night when services were held. My grandfather would also go and pray for a child in the family. I was conceived. My father knew a local saintly figure in Gwalior who used to follow this sadhu or Fakir. One day, this Fakir turned around and asked my father why he was always following him, especially when his desire to have a child was about to be fulfilled through the Kunwar Baba Temple!

This Fakir, in essence, was declaring that my parents would soon have a child. These are the conditions under which I was born and named Kunwar Prasad because I was a blessing from Kunwar Baba. This is how I was named. The Temple's holy men touched the ceremonial sword to my head and declared that I would be safe from any being. This was amply proved repeatedly when there were occasions of great danger to my life. These will be added later on.

Returning to my father, he was an office assistant in the Scindia secretariate at Miti Mahal Palace, Gwalior. The office was of the Gas and Boiler Inspector. His boss was Virendra Sahai Saxena, an impeccable man dressed in western clothes down to the hat. This boss and the head clerk of the office used to bother my father, who was not fluent in English. They kept troubling him throughout his life of work in the office until he retired (he took the retirement himself because of his age and uncontrollable high blood pressure).

Once, I took the courage to meet Virendra Sahai Saxena in his office, pleading to deal with my father gently because he was in poor health. My father's office was transferred from Gwalior to Ujjain for several years, and everybody moved. But, by then, we were six brothers and one sister (I being the eldest). My mother and all the children stayed in Gwalior; my father moved to Ujjain (initially, only I was left behind in Gwalior for my studies, and everyone moved; then, after a year or so, they all came back). During that period of living alone, cooking twice a day, walking a long distance to his office on foot, etc., he continued to decline in his health. On another occasion, during his visit from Ujjain, he brought a large container of perhaps ten or fifteen pounds of laddus that he had made with the help of his orderly, and he carried that gift for all of his family, which I still remember. One day, his orderly sent me a message that I should take my father back to Gwalior. I ran to Ujjain, saw him in sad shape, and wrote a letter to his boss that I was taking him home because he was severely sick. It was kind of a very effective resignation. At home, he was at least under the care of my mother, and I was employed in the central library, providing some source of sustenance. Once before, I visited my father at Ujjain. He entertained me well with whatever best he could, but his own life could be far from what it was. I was embarrassed that I couldn't do much to assist my father; after all, I was still a child at the time.

My father was a statistician. He told me that he was used to calculations containing numerous figures without any calculating machines and only in his mind by looking at those figures. Every morning, after his prayers, which used to be very long, I felt he was reciting Hanuman Chalisa 107 times daily. This prayer has 40 lines in it, and no matter how fast it is recited, it still takes three to four minutes for recitation. So, after taking his brunch, he would walk to his office, which was at least four to five miles from our residence. He used to take very long strides. He walked all his life and declined to use a bicycle, which he never learned to ride. It is surprising, now that I think about it, that none of his friends, such as Majhle Chacha, Raghunath Swaroop Bhatnagar, or Sukhdev Sahai Saxena, ever rode a bicycle. He was an avid walker and walked seven to eight miles one way to the Mela grounds to watch the Scindia Gold Cup Hockey Tournament yearly, in which teams of renown were invited to play.

I remember the name "Dhyan Chand" as one of the greatest players the field of hockey has known. Our Temple was also at least seven miles from our home, and every Monday evening, all of our family would walk that distance for the service and return in the early hours of Tuesday morning. Nearly a hundred or more devotees would attend that service. I will add an entirely new Temple section to this account.

My father was the composer of prayer-full poetry praising the deities at the Temple. He composed some 80 such prayers, which were set to rhythms (Raga and Ragini). He used to play the tambourine and would sing these at the Temple. I copied them and gave them to my brothers. He had another faculty, and that was memorization. He had the entire Ramayana by Tulsidas in his memory. On-demand, if you give him a word or two from anywhere in this big book, he will complete the reference to the context of those lines. He was an avid chess player and used to say that nobody could be beaten more than 99 times!

Among his friends were people like Mr. Bhave and Mr. Atmaram Bhati. The latter gave me shelter and food when my parents and family were away in Ujjain. That was for over a year. I was not employed by the Central Library yet.

He was always in poor health. He suffered from asthma because he smoked locally made cigarettes (called Bidis). The holy men at the Temple once offered to substitute good health with the Bhakti (devotion) he carried. My father politely declined the restoration of his health for this exchange! He was a member of the Dev Samiti, so I am with my brothers to this day. He suffered from high blood pressure that was never under control. He used to take Serpina tablets for his blood pressure. Once, he showed symptoms of paralysis of the hypoglossal nerve; his tongue protruded and deviated to one side. He recovered after a few days in the hospital. His cousin, Chatur Behari Lal Bhatnagar, had him in Allahabad for medical treatment of his condition several times. I was very attached to this grand old man, whom I called Tau Ji. He was a great writer and influenced me with his personality. He had one son, Ajai (Munne), who died young, perhaps in his fifties, of a brain tumor operated on but could not be removed completely. Ajai had five sisters.

Chatur Behari Tau Ji was married (a second time) to the sister of Raghunath Swaroop Chacha's third wife. My dadi (grandmother) was the sister of Beni Kishan Bhatnagar of Agra, who had a daughter, Krishna (Lallo), who lived with Raghunath Swaroop Chacha's family and called him Mama Ji. I have to ask someone about the relationship. It may be that Beni Kishan Bhatnagar's sister married Raghunath Swaroop. Krishna, or Lallo, was the daughter of Beni Kishan.

On the fateful day of my father's passing, I was with my family in Guna, and Kailash (the next oldest brother) was visiting his in-laws in Allahabad. Only Mahesh (the next-in-line brother) was at home. That morning, my father had tea and told my mother to cook dal for him while he went out in the neighborhood for his morning visits. He returned home at about 11 and went to take a bath. My mother heard a loud 'RAM' from him; he passed away. Our mausa Ji, Ram Kishore, a homeopath, was summoned, who declared him dead. Dr. Bisaria called my college at Guna and gave me the startling news, and we all left by the next available bus, arriving, as I recall, in time for his cremation that same evening (February 16, 1966). My mother lived some 20 years longer. She was with my brother Mahesh at Ratlam, where my brother Kailash had transferred her from his home in Gwalior. Mahesh returned home late at night on my mother's fateful day. My mother commented, "Beta, tum aa gaye!" (Son, you have arrived!). These were her last words; she was dead in her sleep the following morning.

I had taken many walking trips with my father, Badri Mama Ji, and Majhle chacha, not all together, but one by one. My favorite place where I would walk with any of them was the Hanuman Takri, a temple of Lord Hanuman on a high hill, some 1000 feet tall and visible from our house. We will wake up early and walk for 25 minutes, climbing the hill. Stay there a while and then come down. I have often taken my books to this Temple, sat there, and studied for hours during exam times. On other occasions, I would double ride the bicycle with my father and take him several longer miles to other temples. He was very fond of such activities. There are many, many temples that I still visit upon reaching Gwalior.

In 1965, I was in correspondence with American universities for my graduate education. My father had asked me not to leave India and him before he passed. He died in February 1966, and I sat foot in Buffalo, New York, on January 6, 1967, alone, having left Indu, Divya, and Jyoti in Gwalior/Dehradun. My father was once selected as the best secretary in Maharaja Scindia's entire secretariate. Pitaji was invited to the Dashera Durbar, where he presented a gold Ginni (sovereign) to the Maharajah at Court, and he was honored by a Sanad (gold embossed certificate signed "J. M. Scindia") and a black Waterman fountain pen. I used the pen later, and I must have "destroyed" it by misuse.

Among foods, Pita Ji, like his father and sons, was also a gourmet cook. He used to enjoy different foods, especially sweets. Once, he told me that upon being challenged, he consumed over 40 Gulab Jamuns in one sitting, and that too after eating a full meal! One of his friends with whom he used to sing was "Khema." The latter's wife used to sell chudis, and we called her Chudiwali Aunty. Despite being an excellent walker, Pita Ji, for many years, used to do regular morning exercises at home.

In Gwalior, we changed many homes. I recall these in order: I was born in the house on Bawan Paiga (rented from Shambhu Ji) in 1934. Then we moved to a house behind the Janakganj Hanuman Ji, then we moved to the Saxena home I mentioned where my Babaji died. We moved to Bakshi-Ki-Goth (Babu Lal Bhatnagar's rental home) adjacent to Raghunath Chacha Ji's house (also a rental), then to Jasoos Mahal, a rental house near the electric station in Bhau-Ka-Bazar, behind the Markandeshwar Temple. We purchased the house in Saki-Baki-Ki-Goth from this rental home in 1947, which sheltered our family for decades. It was my mother who, despite her less than limited means, added many rooms and renovated the house many times. Now that everyone has moved out, we look forward to selling it. It will vend with great difficulty since it has no front. Our family was always treated cruelly by the neighbor, who sold this property to us, Madan Mohan Sharma, since deceased, but only after giving his traits to his sons; the saga continues. I pray that the house will be sold soon so that my brothers will be relieved of undue pressure.

Pita Ji was the only son. He had a sister, "Narayani." As luck would be against her, she was married into a very cruel family. Pita Ji talked to me a few times about how his sister was tortured to death.

His uncle, Ishwari Sahai, had five sons and a daughter; most of them settled in Moradabad; the eldest, Brahma Swaroop Bhatnagar, came to Shivpuri and became a teacher, living their entire lifetime in this city. He was closest to me. I visited him for several summers before I went to high school. The family would take care of me nicely, despite their limited means. My father was transferred to Shivpuri and moved us, his whole family, for a year or more. We were renting a bullet home just outside of the boundary of Shivpuri. There was an old oil mill there. Discovering the pouring sesame seeds from a natural spout, we, young children, used to feed upon a fistful of the delicious sesame seeds. This building still stands, and one can see it on the Agra-Bombay Road either entering or leaving Shivpuri towards Gwalior. It was here in the house I had returned from Gwalior after an incident at our Temple where I almost died because I had gone to sleep standing while on 'duty' at the time of service. Suddenly, I shrieked loudly, uncontrolled, as though in a stance. I was turning pale every moment. My father put me before the holy man we call 'Maharaj' who gave me a Jhadni (aired me with a bunch of peacock feathers) saying the only words 'Sota Hai' meaning "he sleeps"! I was in severe ill health for several weeks after this incident. I had a high fever and hallucinations. I returned to Shivpuri in this condition; I still had a high fever, and on the plastered walls, I imagined an entire play involving tiny creatures, people, etc. I have read this feverish condition and its name and symptoms in a dictionary, but I do not recall them at the moment. Could it be delirium? For numerous years, I have had and continue to have such nightmares, which hit me hard soon after I sleep. Why I initially shrieked for several minutes will not be known, but it is conjectured that because I was derelict in my duty, I was to be taught a lesson by the guarding spirits at the service. Now and then, there would be many so-called mentally imbalanced people wailing loudly at the service. No explanations can be offered other than just conjectures.

At the Temple, Pita Ji used to carry the pleas and prayers of female devotees to Maharaj, who would be sitting inside the Temple. No women were allowed to climb up. This would be done for several hours; the service would end just before dawn, and everyone would depart. My father would walk directly to his office, and in 9th and 10th grade, I would stop at my high school on the way. Despite an almost sleepless Monday night, it was tough to stay awake at school. This service has been going on there without interruption since at least 1925 through this day.

My mother, Bhagwati Devi Bhatnagar

*A sketch drawn by Dr. KP Bhatnagar on May 15ᵗʰ 1961 in a
letter written to his wife.*

My mother would carry the tiffin for my father
because he would walk miles from his office. When I
reached high school (9th and 10th grades), which was close
to the school, I did the same, where my mother was carrying
dinner for both of us—my father and I—and most of the
time, my mother would be fasting, eating only after midnight
when Savari came to the Gadhhi. But in between, she did not
forget to feed me and buy an additional piece of sweets from

Rao Sahib's shop, who was also the Darbar poet (Bhaat). When Savari came, he was the first to recite a prayer praising Kunwar Baba: "Naam Let so katat Kalesh Dev Sevak Bhavani ko, Saritar samir neer ulte bahai det haarat par peer surati savani ko, naam let so katat kalesa dev Sevak Babhani ko." One or two other such small prayers will be offered; Darbar (another name for Kunwar Baba) Sahib will give "Bataashas" to these courtiers, and the routine of a kingly Darbar will commence. I would like to describe Darbar's semblance to the Darbar of Prithviraj Chauhan's times.

For a mother, all children are alike, but my mother, Mataji, had six sons and a daughter (me, the eldest; sister, Raj Kumari; brothers-Kailas (deceased as of this printing), Ganesh (deceased), Mahesh, Chanda, and Kishan), I was the dearest to her. She would always treat me with special consideration, food, and blessings. It was her hard work that played a decisive role in my life. Everything centered around me resulted from that moment when she took me to a distant uncle of mine, Har Kishore Bhatnagar, Professor of Physics at the local Victoria College, requesting him to get me admitted to the first-year science biology class. It happened that way, and my fate has smiled on me ever since. It was tough for her to lose her husband, and the next year, in January 1967, I left for the United States. Indu, Divya, and Jyoti joined me in June 1968. Then I was under the loving care of Indu, who helped me complete my Ph.D. We were recruited at the University of Louisville School of Medicine, Department of Anatomy by Professor James B. Longley, the chairman.

Mataji was the third of four sisters and two brothers. All of these six families were growing up and were settled in Gwalior. Mataji used to stitch clothes for us using the sewing machine of her elder sister, wife of Ram Prasad Bhatnagar. She had a son and seven daughters, all educated through Master's level and one daughter taking an MD degree. The younger sister, Gayadei (married to Ram Kishore Airania, an art teacher, painter, photographer, homeopath, a great artist, and a humanist I have known), had three sons and two daughters. Her eldest son is Anand Prakash, MD, a neurologist in Corona, California. This cousin is the dearest to me. My mother visited us in the USA in 1974 and stayed for four months. Gayadei Mausi and Ram Kishore Mausaji also visited us in the Kings Hwy, Louisville house. When I was living alone in Gwalior, collecting rent of a few rupees from my other eldest Mausaji, Shyam Swaroop Bhatnagar (husband of my mother's eldest sister), who was renting our Saki-Baki-Ki-Goth house. Ram Kishore Mausa Ji happily gave me three rupees for several months to live on. At that time, I lived in a rental room at Ghosibada in Chatri Bazar and went to school in the Science-Math program at the Intermediate College in Jayendraganj, Gwalior. This room had nothing else but a room. A class fellow of mine, perhaps Mr. Jha or Barua, who lived close by, had given me the privilege of using their bathroom for the facilities. I lived there for several months and then moved to the next location. I lived with Atma Ram Bhati and his family for a while in Naya Bazar. During this period, I came to cherish this family. He also rented a room in Nai Sarak. He lived with Shankar Pandit (Badri Mamma Ji's priest, Bal Kishan Sharma's son from Jora Alapur), who was going through college education in Gwalior. I cannot recall the exact sequence of my living at these various places in those few years when my father was moving, on transfer, from Gwalior to Shivpuri, to Ujjain, etc. Once I left Gwalior on appointment to Hamidia College, Bhopal (within 40 days or so, I was transferred to the College of Science, Raipur through the chance courtesy of the Education Secretary, MP Government, Bhopal, whom I met at the market and subsequently visited his office. I asked him if I should stay in academia (but I did not like my posting at the Intermediate College, Bhopal) or take up a research position at one of the institutes in Lucknow. He told me to stay in academia and promptly transferred me to Raipur, where the beginnings of my career took shape. I stayed at Raipur for two years, then transferred to Holkar College, Indore, and then to Government College, Jhabua, where I brought my bride, Indu, and after one year, was moved to Guna, closer to Gwalior, in 1962. By 1966, I was getting ready to be on study leave going to the USA. I would like to describe these segments of my life in detail elsewhere. The strongest influence on my life and that of my siblings happened to be from our mother. My father did not care for anything other than the daily business of earning bread as long as he could, and the rest of the time was devoted to worship. It is a great surprise that despite our household's very low monthly income, my mother was running the expenses, maintaining her own house, and, in small measures, saving regularly. Toward the end of her period, she, with Kailash's assistance, distributed all of her material wealth to our brothers. It consisted of some jewelry and a good amount of cash. I do not think we got anything gifted to us from our grandparent's side. My mother was tireless, always busy doing something, never wasting a moment. On numerous occasions, I would arrive in the Temple's early morning hours and be hungry. She would start the wood fire and make me quick snacks. Anytime any guest would arrive at our house, she would cook a full meal for the guest, regardless of the time of the day or the evening. She used to invite her senior relatives to come and be our house guests for a few days. We regularly received Taiji (Omkari Bibi's mother, my grandfather's sister, Sarsuti, from Allahabad or Bijnor, and Brahma Chacha from Shivpuri). She hardly bought anything for herself and would be the last one to serve herself from the leftovers, many times not enough for this last person, but she will not cook another meal for herself. She would remain hungry until the next meal time. Her health was frail.

She was very attached to her eldest daughter-in-law, Indu, and their first grandchildren, Divya and Jyoti. She was a fantastic cook, creating dish after dish from minimum supplies. She came to the States with us in 1974 and stayed for four months. She had no objection to serving non-vegetarian dishes on the dinner table, while she was a total vegetarian. With enthusiasm, she served her in-laws and later admirably her husband, who controlled the number of cigarettes he could smoke in one day. When she would be going to a celebration in our family, it was my duty to either get all of my family dressed up and be taken to the household, or if dinner was to be at home, then I was to keep everything ready in the kitchen so that my mother, no sooner than she would arrive, could begin the preparation of meals. In those days, I used to think that in our kitchen, there ought to be several small containers each for different ingredients, such as oils, sugar, flour, salt, lentils, rice, and so on. Even Indu, over several years, cooked using wood as fuel. Then came coal and sawdust. Natural gas came much later.

In 1971, she undertook a pilgrimage with people from our Temple at Gwalior. These were Shinde Sahib, his mother, Gaya Prasad Srivastava, his wife, my mother, and a few others. They reached Haridwar and then systematically walked or took the available transportation to the four great Dhams – Gangotri, Yamunotri, Kedarnath, and Badrinath, returning to Haridwar and Gwalior. She wrote me a letter on the tree bark in those snowy heights and brought Gangotri water for us. These are preserved at our home here. Later, we would visit these pilgrimage sites and remember our ancestors who had gone through the same steps a million times and through thousands of generations. I wonder if my line is stopped because we moved to the United States. My daughters and their families will have the least desire to go on such trips and will not know such attempts' physical and spiritual benefits. Until now, we have always gone to Haridwar for bathing in the holy Ganges whenever we visit India.

Last year, in March 2005, when Indu and I reached New Delhi, two weeks ahead of Jyoti and her family's arrival there for two weeks, Preeti was very sick. Within the first few days, Indu, I, and Shobha didi took a trip to

Hardwar-Rishikesh, stayed at Parmarth Niketan for a night, and bathed in the Ganges. Preeti passed away on the 16th of March. It was with Preeti, Krishna, Annu and family, and Meetu that we went on the pilgrimage of Badrinath and

Kedarnath in the 1980s.

My marriage and how I got engaged

Dr. Divya Cantor

A sketch drawn by Dr. KP Bhatnagar on May 15th 1961 in a letter to Indu.

After I completed my Master's, I began to get proposals for my marriage. One of the first ones was from Dehradun. Many more came later on, and none were suitable for my parents. As for me, I was willing to wait for a scientist's daughter. None surfaced, and they were lost between two and three years. Seeing nothing on the horizon to fulfill my wishes, I told my father to enquire from the family at Dehradun if the young Indu was still unengaged. She was. We were soon engaged, and then little pieces of information began to surface. Indu's father, Mr. Brahma Shankar Varma, was a research chemist (B.Sc, Lahore) and a published researcher (1925–1984). He had some patented procedures, such as making a big camphor cake from plant products. We (he and I) began to converse, telling him that I was interested in research on bats. He, by then, had found a position with Col RN Chopra at the Regional Research Laboratory, Jammu and Kashmir, working on drug uses for Indian medicinal plants. He got me four fruit bats preserved and sent them to me. The resulting research on those bats (OS Penis of the Indian Megachiroptera, J Mammalogy, 1967) was my second peer-reviewed paper and acknowledges Mr. Varma's help getting those bats. His cousin was married to Sir Shanti Swaroop Bhatnagar, a noted chemist, and creator of the National Research Laboratories, with the help of Pandit Jawahar Lal Nehru. A story within a story, as in the Arabian Nights. Once at either Oxford or Cambridge, the three future scientists – Sir

Shanti Swaroop, Homi Jahangir Bhabha, and Megh Nath Saha – were preparing a meal when King George VI happened to pass by and was greeted by the trio. The King readily accepted the dinner invitation (from The Biography of Sir Shanti Swaroop). Another anecdote: My professor, Dr. Shyama Charan Srivastava, one day was dressed in a blue woolen suit. I complimented him on how smart he looked in that apparel. Years after that, I chose a near similar suit color. Someone complimented me but asked if there was any reason for me to select that particular color. I responded that it was "For wearing when presenting myself before my professor in America." There was no trace of my going to America. I was mentioning that, BUT it happened exactly like I said-I wore that suit before Dr. Kallen, my future mentor, in Buffalo, New York. I am tempted to add a few more incidents. In 1958, I was first appointed as a lecturer at Hamidia College, Bhopal, and was transferred to the College of Science, Raipur, after 40 days. There I was lecturing. Suddenly I was stopped mid-sentence. I walked out to see the room number, which was the same in which I was lecturing in my dream! I was forewarned about the incident. I was in Guna, whereas Indu was to give birth to Divya and two years later to Jyoti in Gwalior. In both cases, I dreamt of the two daughters in the night or two before the birth. At the time of my wedding, I met his elder brother, Dr. Rama Shankar Varma, MD (Oxford, England), Professor of Ophthalmology at Agra Medical College. I had a very pleasant and intelligent conversation with him.

After receiving the Master's degree in Zoology from Vikram University (I am the very first Master's graduate of

Vikram University; I do not know if my name is on their honor roll!), I was first appointed in Bhopal and soon transferred to Raipur. In Bhopal, I met my life-long best friend, Kripa Shankar Saxena (to be written about), and moved to a post-graduate college, which was well served by academic faculty. There was Dr. DharamVir Ramratan Sharma, a lecturer, who soon received promotions that were well deserved and with whom I became friendly. His research was published in foreign journals. His thesis artist was now employed at the Regional Research Laboratory, Jammu and Kashmir, the place where my future father-in-law was also posted. This was the connection that eventually, Mr. Brahma Shankar Varma (my father-in-law) and Raj Dulari, my mother-in-law, got to propose to their youngest daughter, Indu Bala Bhatnagar, for marriage to me. The other recommendation came from Majhle Chachaji, Raghunath Swaroop Bhatnagar, who was attending his nephew's wedding with Shobha Bhatnagar, the third daughter of BS Varma, and was watching the admirable young girl, Indu, who seemed to be at the center of all actions. He liked Indu very much and recommended that our family consider the relationship. Not knowing the Varma family of Dehradun and now of Jammu and Kashmir, on my own, I was attempting to sort through several dozen proposals for me to find out if there was a suitable girl of scientific parentage. In this process, Indu's proposal was first. Three years were to elapse when I told my parents that I was not getting any younger; no proposal as I would like was in clear view, so let us open up the very first proposal. On my prompting, my father enquired of Varmaji if Indu was still unmarried and if they would

consider the relationship. Within 15 days, we were
traveling to New Delhi for negotiations. I was to see Indu at
their cousin Govind Shankar's Bhatnagar. The families got
together; I saw Indu's glimpse in a mirror (just like
Alauddin Khilzi, the Mugal emperor, meeting Padmini
indirectly through the mirror, a historical fact); later, she
served refreshments. Indu's mother gave her own "gold
ring" to be recast into a present to me. I have regretted
receiving that gift in that form since why would I let my
mother-in-law be deprived of her own jewelry? At that
time, I could not say anything. This happened in December
1960. We were married on April 28, 1961, in Dehradun.
The wedding was attended by ChaturBehari Tauji, Badri
Mamaji, and my sick father, among other relatives.

At the time of my wedding, I was at Holkar
College, Indore, on transfer to Jhabua College, where I took
Indu for the first time. She was a very young girl, but she
suited herself for all the tasks of establishing a household.
Jhabua was a princely state, small and tribal. There were
two temples we were fond of visiting often, etc. One of the
Shiva Temples was on the way to the college, where I
walked every day from home. That was the ideal location
for the temple, next to a pond and several huge shade trees,
such as Peepal. I would stop there for prostrations. Another
was the Hanuman Temple on a hill, where on Tuesdays and
or Saturdays, Indu and I used to go for evening darshan.
My brother Chanda was living with us and going to
college. There was the local Randive family we knew well.
In front of our house, rented from Sethji, there was a
lawyer family, the Srivastavas, whom we had made friends

with. Our two-room apartment with a verandah and second-floor house was our first. We invited the principal of Holkar College, Dr. Bhagwat, and other colleagues for afternoon tea when they were attending a reception at the college.

Among our friends at Jhabua were the Kheras (who moved to England), Dr. and Mrs. Jain, Mr. Kelkar, Mr. Vajpai (Principal), and the Hindi Professor. By chance, K. S. Saxena was assigned as a Forest Range Officer in Jhabua. His company was always good. On Sundays, there used to be a tribal market. There was another Temple in the main bazaar, next to the Jhabua palace gate. This was a crude copy of the Khajuraho Temple, explicitly exhibiting sexual postures on the outer walls. It was small. I had gone inside the Jhabua palace to collect bats. One night, there was a big storm.

Walking to college, I discovered fallen tree limbs from which were still hanging dozens of *Pteropus*, the giant fruit-eating bats, and females suckling young ones. These are the most difficult species to collect, yet there was a field of them there for hand-picking. I collected ten or more animals and reached college with both hands full. On the way, I found a big tortoise that was picked too. All these animals were preserved and might still be in the collection of the zoology department. However, I wanted to return to good old Jhabua, but I never have. The desire is still there. There was a lady doctor who helped Indu a great deal. I believe Indu had an early miscarriage of some four weeks or so. When my mother came for a visit, she was sick for many days. The lady doctor helped her a great deal too. There was the young Deputy Collector we had begun to know. There was an officer's club. We used to play bridge, but not at the club. Several times, we took a trip by bus to Meghnagar, a town bordering Jhabua and the state of Gujarat. The very large, dark Gulab jamuns were a great delicacy there. We used to travel to Jhabua by bus from Indore and travel nearly all night, arriving in the morning. There was no public transport other than a few four-wheeled carts. The entire city of Jhabua could be walked in less than an hour. There were only a few streets and lots of monkeys.

It was learned much later after marriage that my desire to be married into a scientist's family had been realized. My father-in-law, BS Varma, was a chemist-scientist who published his first paper in 1924 and the last book in collaboration with Colonel Chopra of the Regional Research Laboratory of Jammu and Kashmir in 1974. There were many papers and some inventions, such as how to make a cake of camphor during production. He was a member of the scientific elite at the Forest Research Institute, Dehradun. He got me four bats collected and preserved from Jammu. Because of these bats, I published my third paper while still living in India and preparing to leave for the USA. At one point, he had recommended me to Dr. ML Roonwal, a former scientist at the FRI (Forest Research Institute), Dehradun, and later a scientist at one of the research institutes in Calcutta. This working relationship did not flourish because of the distance. Indu's elder brother, Gopal Bhai, was an MMS, MD from Lucknow. He died in a freak accident of drowning in a river while shooting and retrieving birds! Indu's brother, Krishna, is a chemical engineer and a specialist in industrial oils and wax production. He is credited with the establishment of numerous factories in his field. Indu's eldest sister, Shashi (married to J D Singh), passed away last year (Nov 2005) while Indu was visiting India for Adu's wedding in New Delhi. The other two sisters and their families are Ravi didi and KIP Bhatnagar, Chandigarh, Shobha didi, and Jagdish Swaroop Bhatnagar, New Delhi. This family is terrific and must be divine, for they have many solid attributes.

Those few trips I made to Dehradun are deeply embedded in my mind. I liked the stay, the visits, picnics, Sulphur Spring, temples, walks, and meeting friends and relatives. I remember only once going to Mussorie but coming back the same day. Indu has many relatives living in Dehradun, and her aunt (Jitendra's mother) is living through her 100th year. Her Tauji, Dr. RS Varma, MD Ophthalmology Professor at Agra Medical College, had spent some ten years in England on a military commission.

Descended from Indu and me are our two physician daughters, Divya (Ob-Gyn) and Jyoti (Dermatologist), with their very bright kids, Alec Vishal Rouben for Divya and Cami (Nina Camille) Burruss, Matthew Prasad Burruss and Clayton Prakash Burruss for Jyoti.

Excursions into Research – the Original Investigations

A sketch drawn by Dr. KP Bhatnagar on May 29th 1961 in a letter with his poem to Indu.

प्यार हो जाता स्वयं ही।

यह किया जाता नहीं॥

वारि के बदले बरसृता बादलो से हो अमृत।

स्वाति के अतरक्षित चातक से पिया जाता नहीं॥

Love happens by itself.

It doesn't need to be done.

If it is raining nectar from the clouds instead of water.

Even in the most suitable moments the bird can't drink it. The desire to delve into independent research investigations in the life sciences originated during my tenure at the College of Science Raipur. I was greatly influenced by the ongoing research program by Dr. Sharma and Ms. Saraswati Sivaram Iyer. While eager to assist me, Dr. Sharma did not have much time for my research scholar training. It was due to my not being very strong about the issue. Things were kind of dredging. Some miles away from the college and our bungalow, there was this village, Sarona. Between two lovely ponds, a great, ancient Shiva Temple and another small temple, where the statue of poet-saint Tulsidas was installed. I used to visit this place nearly once a week, perhaps on Mondays. It was here that I fervently prayed, especially on a Shivratri day, that Shiva may help me with my desire to conduct research. I began collecting that day – I collected spiders, and there used to be a great colony of an insect, *Sphrocephala hiersiana*, who had eyes on long stalks. I have never sat silent since that day, in February 1959. There is always a project or two in the making, and so are the divine blessings of Lord Shiva in my life. I took these insects to the laboratory and attempted to grow them to study their cycle, but I was unsuccessful in that effort. I had another colleague, Raj Krishna Khanna, who is still a good friend of mine. He kindly let me be his co-author on the abstract on the cardiac conduction system of the crow; this was submitted and read at the Indian National Congress. Dr. Ravi Prakash, chairman at the Bhopal Postgraduate College, was a big name at that time in zoology, and many students would work with him on the heart.

I remember an incident when I may have been in the sixth or seventh grade, studying science at Gorkhi Middle School, Lashkar. At a friend's house in Janakganj, we set up a small distillation apparatus in one corner of the room. The spirit lamp was lighted, and within a few minutes, we had a small explosion instead of distilled water, with all our "equipment" turning into fine pieces! Several years later, when I was in college studying biology, I was fascinated by having a microscope of my own. My maternal uncle was a chemist with the local municipal laboratory. He was used to analyzing milk and other food products. He had an expensive compound microscope, which I used sparingly in his laboratory. He had an expensive compound microscope which I used sparingly in his laboratory. This was the scope that I wanted to be reproduced. So, I found a first-rate mechanic, took the microscope with my uncle's permission, and let him examine the issue. In a few days, he told me that he could mold everything else, but the optical components of the microscope could not be built by him. That was the end of my own microscope.

Who knew then that I would work with world-class microscopes, from ordinary dissecting to compound, research, and various types of microscopes in the USA and Germany? I developed an improvised microfilm reader from my so-called research explorations in Guna, which I fashioned from a low-power magnifying device. This was my first note, which I sent to Turtox News, Chicago. They published it and even sent me 200 reprints for free. I was running wild in the streets, showing off my friends my first reprint of a paper published in the USA! Were there clouds gathering to take me over my home country to the USA? For it was not more than a year or two that I set out to face uncertainties, but my blessings and the angels still with me continue to turn the tides always in my favor.

Dr. Sharma gave me a project to work up original findings on the baculum (penis bone or os penis). In Jhabua, I had four bats, preserved and sent to me by my father-in-law from Jammu, that were male specimens, Pteropids, which I had collected from the damaging storm. The penis was removed. I followed the methods from a published paper (also in Turtox News) for making transparent alizarin preparations. Using a mild solution of potassium hydroxide and sunlight on the window sill, this project slowly developed into a full-length report, which I dared to submit to the Journal of Mammalogy in Kansas, USA! With a minor revision, it was published in the journal as a real paper in 1967, when I arrived in Buffalo. This time my enthusiasm remained confined to the halls of the medical school, where even one or two faculty members were surprised at this novice from India, already publishing a paper in one of the hard-liner journals! While in Guna, while dissecting a leech, I discovered duplications of the reproductive system. Promptly enough, a paper was written. I invited my junior, Anil Kumar Srivastava, a lecturer in Zoology (to review).

This paper was published in Current Science, Bangalore, India, before I left for the USA. I will now begin a real intensive course of study for about five years before attempting to publish my research, but then I will never stop until I retire and possibly beyond.

Numerous people have asked me why I chose to work on bats! The primary reasons were my angels or Dr. Shyamacharan, my professor for my six years in college. Both Drs. SCS and Shiv Sahai were getting their Ph. D.s, as I was in the first year of science-biology. Dr. SCS had his Ph.D. on the placenta of the Indian mouse-tailed bat, *Rhinopoma microphyllum.* I adored Dr. SCS so much that I looked forward to researching bats from then on. Dr. SCS had a beautiful blue woolen suit in which he looked very classy. I would not be left behind, and when my time came to buy a suit piece for me at the time of my marriage, I selected one of the best pieces and had a suit stitched.

During my marriage, I was even asked by my in-laws (Dr. Rama Shankar Verma) what I wanted to achieve by dressing so elegantly. Promptly came my response that I would wear this suit when I saw my American professor for the first time. In 1961, when I was married and conversing, there was not even a dream that I would ever visit the USA, so I was bragging, if not lying! But, given six more years, I was wearing the same suit when I met my future angel and mentor, Dr. Frank Clements Kallen, in Buffalo, New York! This is the story of the blue woolen suit and why I chose to work with bats. Anything I ever did with bats was the first of its kind since there are not as many bat morphologists as there are fingers on the human hand! And I am one of them, having published on various topics ranging from bat anatomy to comparisons with humans and other primates. I have often said that only a comparative anatomist is the real scientist on the scene and that knowledge that is either limited to human anatomy or animal anatomy remains incomplete.

Speaking of angels, what have they given me? I used to travel by bus from Gwalior to Bhopal, Indore, or the South. I will always cross a tree-lined street in Guna, which I admired most and would look forward to seeing each time there was an opportunity. Lo and behold, I was transferred to Guna in 1962 and stayed there until January 1967 before leaving for the USA. My desire is fulfilled! I got married to the daughter of a scientist who was a near relative of Sir Shanti Swaroop Bhatnagar, FRS (London), the chemist-scientist who created the National Laboratory System in India. My wish was to work on bats, which I proposed while being in India itself. From my reviews, I also determined that I should be working on the sense of smell, for so little was known even in the 1960s on this subject. And, I made myself somebody internationally known in his field of research- chemoreception.

My angels must have thought I wasn't up to par for them to grant me my nearly first serious desire when I was in high school: to leave home in search of spirituality! Had I been successful, I would have troubled my parents for the rest of their lives because they would have lost their first-born son, who was gifted to them from the temple of Sri

Kunwar Maharaj and Kaila Maharani. I had a boyhood friend, a buddy, in Mahendra Nath Saxena (Rajjan), son of Madho Singh Saxena, a magistrate in Gwalior. Rajjan and I used to go to our temple regularly, attending service with my family on Monday nights. Rajjan had been volunteering at the temple for many years. He was losing his mind at times, so it seemed. He was sent to Solan, Punjab, for high school for a while, but he did not improve. A day came when he was nowhere to be found anymore. Maybe he left for the mountains and became a hermit. In that period, he and I both read a lot of literature dealing with the occult and the philosophy of the Hindu religion. I even wrote to the great Swami Sivananda in Rishikesh to allow me a personal interview. I did receive a response in a postcard from his secretary, "First, learn the meaning of attachment and detachment." That response somehow cooled my spirits. Was it for good or not for anybody's good? Who can tell? I still have Rajjan's last communication from Solan to me. That is a postcard.

From my college days, I had grown accustomed to organizing field trips for the class of students. As many as 25 students and one or two professors will ride out on bicycles, and we will roam outside the city limits, exploring the fauna and flora and collecting specimens that will be studied in the lab later. A carriage will carry our picnic goods. Food was sometimes cooked at our destination. Thus, we made several trips to Tighra dam, west of Lashkar and about 12 miles away. This method of studying nature has always stayed with me for all these years. I will describe many of the field trips I organized, wherever I was. These were extremely useful for the research, learning, and teaching atmosphere they provided.

The Big Cats of Bajrang garh, Guna

One weekend, I took out my BSc classes, a group of 20 students, boys and a few girls, all on bicycles. Our goal was to reach the ruins of the Bajranggarh castle, some 10-12 miles east of Guna, and explore the surroundings, even looking for bat roosts, then come down to the village, go to some other dilapidated buildings, an old temple, then go on to the Goddess temple, then by the afternoon, assemble in the garden, cook and rest. So, we were roaming the ruins. I entered one of the darkest and deepest parts of the continuous row of big rooms. I suddenly came upon partially eaten cattle, fresh. Only a tiger had the strength to drag the animal deep and away from every disturbance. We forgot to look for bats and ran out. The tiger might have been hiding in the neighborhood. The rest of the day was exciting too. We collected *Megaderma lyra* from the temple's corridor, *Taphozous* from the high ceilings of an old building in the marketplace, and at the Devi temple, we received blessings. The image there is not looking straight at all but is slightly angled. That same view was very striking to me, and I have never forgotten that look of blessing from the goddess. It was dusk when we were on our way back home. On another occasion, I took my NCC (National Cadet Corps, Company Alpha) company to this town.

General Pindale, with copies going to my Brigadier and the Principal, the loud-voiced Dr. Pendse.

Miles and miles of gastropod, *Physa*, in a valley close to Shivpuri towards Guna

With my class on a Saturday, we took the commercial bus for a day camp, picnic, and field trip. We stopped at a station and moved in on foot, exploring the terrain. I stumbled upon a field of stones that extended for miles and appeared to be a valley surrounded by not-so-tall mountains. A close inspection revealed that we had come upon a field of gastropod fossils that were all sizes but also all sinistral. We filled all possible bags with these fossilized shells and returned to Guna excited. I have carried these fossils with me to the USA. They are beautiful. At the time, I corresponded with the Harvard Comparative Anatomy Museum and the one in Kansas, but I was unable to generate any outside interest in these fossils.

Snakes, and Snakes everywhere

We were on a religious trip of one day to Hindala, an annual pilgrimage from our temple at Gwalior. We left early in the morning by auto, arriving at Bhadawana by 9 am. After a brief halt for bathing and worship at the Shiva temple, we were to progress on foot for many miles ahead. As we were about to bathe in the natural fall, some 20 feet high, we noticed hundreds of snakes being washed down the fall, into the pool and swimming away from the stream. None of us waited any longer to discover whether they were poisonous or non-poisonous snakes. They may very well have been either cobras or vipers, both deadly!

On another occasion, my classmate and friend Gopal Singh Dogra (we were in the second year Master's program at Gwalior) went out on bicycles toward the fields in Old Gwalior. There we explored a few stones, turning them. Gopal uncovered a viper, and as the snake slithered away fast, Gopal ran after it to catch it by the tail. The snake soon disappeared, and we saved a serious accident of a snake bite that may have resulted from such a wild collecting spree! But all was not over yet. We continued searching, came upon an old well, peeped into it, and, interestingly enough, found a cobra swimming with its hood raised above the water! We decided to catch and carry this deadly snake.

How to? We had nothing with us. So, we found a small village and borrowed an earthen pot, a cover, a long bamboo pole, and some length of rope. The pot was gently cracked and tied with the rope that floated in the well. We coaxed the snake to enter the pot, quickly covered with the lid. We were operating from the edge of the well all this time! The closed pot was gently pulled above the water to let it be emptied of water. Now out, we closed the lid tightly and returned what could be returned to the villagers (there were no onlookers all the time during this operation).

Now I put this pot on the bicycle handle between my hands, and we cycled fast through several miles of crowded markets, reaching our home and depositing this contraption in our study room. We slept in the same room all night. The next day, we chloroformed the snake, transferred it into another container, carried it to the laboratory, showed it around, and dissected it. Its poison gland was bulging with the deadly poison. The snake was several feet long! This specimen may be preserved in the Zoology Museum at the College in Gwalior, as are some other specimens and the huge crane we got shot by Gopal's father, Major Karam Singh, and had taxidermized for our museum.

In Guna, at our residence, there was a common wall between the toilet and the washroom, and at eye level, there was a space housing an electric lamp. I was on the toilet. Indu was bathing. As I stood up, my eyes caught a snake under that bulb. I gently told Indu to immediately come out, slowly but quickly, and not ask any questions. She did it for both of us. That was a small cobra sitting in that warmth. Cobras in India are very common, and some 20,000 plus humans die yearly of snake bites. Beyond these incidents, I have had no contact with snakes, nor would I care to have one. Our professor, Dr. Shyamacharan Srivastava, was an avid and careful "snake-catcher.

Collecting Bats

Initially, I never received instructions on where to look for bats and how to catch them alive. In India, wherever you go, there are always some giant fruit-eating bats, *Pteropus giganteus*, hanging dead on electric wires been electrocuted. Their wing span is over five feet; thus, they singe to their demise when they catch the two wires simultaneously. Their tendons tightly hold the wires, some 30 feet above the ground, and they keep hanging there for months, a common sight. These are the only bats I knew. When in Guna, I sat out, and after several half days of searching with Gopi, I got only one partial skeleton of a microbat. Then I gradually acquired the equipment, butterfly nets on long poles, metal cages to put them in, and so on. So often got my fingers pierced by the bat's sharp teeth, unaware of the rabies problem. Megabats are very gentle, and if not held tight, they will not bite, but the little bats are not so forgiving. They bite hard, but only to get out of your hold.

I started from my home. In the open verandah, spots within the stone poles inhabited by one of the tiniest bats, *Pipistrellus mimus*, a few grams in weight. I used to observe these flying in and out of the tiny opening. These bats seemed to stay parallel to the ground once in the crack and not hang upside down, for there was not that much room inside. That was in Guna.

At our home in Gwalior (Saki-Baki/Sathe-Ki-Goth), right over the small kitchen, there was a very dark storage space separated by a thin stone roof. This section was inhabited by the Indian mouse-tailed bat, *Rhinopoma microphyllum*, which did not mind the heat from the kitchen and the human traffic underneath; they flew in and out at their will. Another place that I saw these species inhabiting in common with human occupants was MN Dharkar's house. In a dilapidated section of the house, dark ruins were colonized by hundreds of *Rhinopoma.* At their house, there was *Scotophilus heathi.* The yellow-bodied bats were roosting in the narrow niches of the supporting stone slabs underneath the second-floor corridors. I am unaware of fruit bats taking residence in the houses; in the open ground outside the living quarters, one could always find colonies of *Pteropus, Cynopterus, and Rousettus.* On several evenings, out on the road and moving not too far away from the ramparts of the Gwalior Fort, I saw a continuous stream of bats for an hour or more. They emerged from the areas where I later collected the *Rhinopoma* bats. The Raja Man Singh Palace in Gwalior Fort has numerous colonies of these bats. Here they have been living for six hundred years or more; huge stone carvings also house these bats and several other molossid bats, such as "*Tadarida.*"

Once, with my students from Holkar College Indore, we took a trip to the BazBahaur-Bhanumati Fort in Mandu, Madhya Pradesh. The fort stretches miles in all directions. There were numerous dungeons returning echoes. Stones tell the history there. We had our hearts filled with the capture of *Hipposideridae* and *Rhinolophidae..* We left their cages

59

in the outer cave area to get a few more. On our return, we did not find a single bat in our cages; we do not know whether we did not latch the cages properly or how else the bats would have escaped! Several hours of work were wasted. We caught a few backs and, this time, brought them with us.

One of the most desirable places for collecting bats was the palace at Datia (some 30 miles outside Gwalior). Some seven species of bats were collected from this palace, which appeared haunted, eight or ten-storied, all dark, deserted, and in full control of wild animals, primarily bats; in its courtyard was a place for public hanging during state times; a huge palace (the King's quarters); and facing it, several hundred meters away, was another small palace for the queen, who would move there to show her displeasure. I had some students live in this town. Once or twice, after the collecting was over, we were invited into their parents' homes and showered with hospitality.

It has been months (April to June 2006) since I have not added anything to my autobiography. For decades, wherever I went, I always carried a preparatory box with me which had the essential dissecting apparatus, vials, fixatives, and other necessary equipment so that if there was a specimen, I could fix the tissues then and there. Once, from Guna, I went to a college (the name escapes me) as an external examiner. Upon asking, I was taken to a small ruin where I collected small pipistrelle-sized bats. They were later sent to the British Museum by JP Hill for identification. Hill wanted me to send more of a certain kind from the same locality; I could not fulfill that promise. It sounded like a new species to me.

Dr. Heinz Stephan of the Max-Planck Institute Germany and I collected the bats in India and Thailand. Stephan, at all times, was seldom interested in anything but his own work, and he would drive all of his team toward that one goal. In Cheng Mai (Thailand), we were taken to a deep green valley, and through that lush vegetation, we eventually climbed up a little hill and found a deep cave. We set up the nets there and came out only to re-enter after the night. A place that had changed to a deadly-looking place where ghosts, snakes, and scorpions, not to mention blood-thirsty leeches, would abound. From that spot, we collected a good-sized bat (perhaps *Rhinolophidae)* which was overgrown in every appendage; the ears were abnormally large, and so were the other body parts. It was queer. The brain was removed carefully at our residence, retaining all other features, and the skin was saved and returned to Bangkok. It turned out that it was the only fourth specimen of that bat species ever caught in Thailand! On another evening, we set up our nets in a vast field of vegetation that was also full of leeches of all sizes. These happened to find the holes at the bottom of my pants and thus crawl onto my body surface, only to be discovered at home where we would undress and our bodies searched by another person for a feeding leech, which had to be cut off by a sharp knife to detach it. There were three leeches on my body and seven on Dr. Stephan's!

Dr. Divya Cantor

I would like to describe our expedition to Mexico in 1976 to bring vampire bats to my laboratory in Louisville. It took months to prepare for the trip since we had to obtain permits from the US and the Mexican governments to export and import these live creatures. I was lucky to have had the guidance from Dr. William Abel Wimsatt of Cornell University and the collegial help from William (Bill) Lopez Forment, who was doing a Master's at Cornell under Wimsatt while I was at Buffalo. Bill Forment had supplied me with live *Artibeus* for my doctoral research. Bill Forment agreed to help us out while we were in Mexico. Our party consisted of myself, Greg Cooper, Leon Kundrotas, and Barry Spoonamore, my three graduate students. We borrowed the university's 16-seater van. We left some seats to make room for luggage and/or sleeping, and we set out from (Saturday, June 19, 1976, to Thursday, July 1, 1976). We drove for three days and three nights, some 3,000 miles one way to Mexico. We were on the road for 18 hours a day, with one person driving some 150 miles and then resting while in motion. We enjoyed the food on the way. Farm-reared cartilaginous fish was plentiful in the restaurants. It took us two and a half days to reach Mexico City; we were staying at the Hotel Escargot. The next day, we left for Veracruz across a wide river, a deep rivulet before the bat cave was reached. William Forment was our guide. The rivulet was crossed after being stripped of our clothes and belongings; the cave was close by. We spent some two hours collecting. Collected and caged were the vampires: Desmodus *rotundus*, two *Diphylla ecaudata, Artibeus jamaicensis, and Carollia perspicillata*. Leaving by the same route, we had to cross a rising river. Our van stalled twice. Fortunately, it started after hitting restart two times. Leon was feverish, but somehow, we reached our hotel in Mexico City. At the hotel, we made contact with Bill Forment by phone, and with him, we organized an expedition to Veracruz the next day or so.

Upon departure, now at the Mexico-US border, a scientist had to be called in to verify the export permit of bats. On the road, we saw a burrow flattened out like cardboard. We drove nonstop for two and a half days to Louisville. On the way, I noticed a Diphylla in parturition! The process was observed, noted, and photographed (subsequently published in J Mammalogy 1978, 59:864-866). The next day, we left for Louisville, driving nonstop. We reached the Louisville lab first and set up bats in separate cages; only then did we reach our residences. Several papers were published in the years to follow, two of which utilized the collected material. The entire effort of the Mexican field trip was extraordinarily paid for. *Carollia bred very well in captivity; Desmodus lived for two years; they were fed one large ice cube made from defibrinated cattle blood collected from the local slaughterhouse.* As long as I had the live vampires, they were to be fed daily, and as a result of the care needed, I did not leave Louisville for even half a day for more than two years.

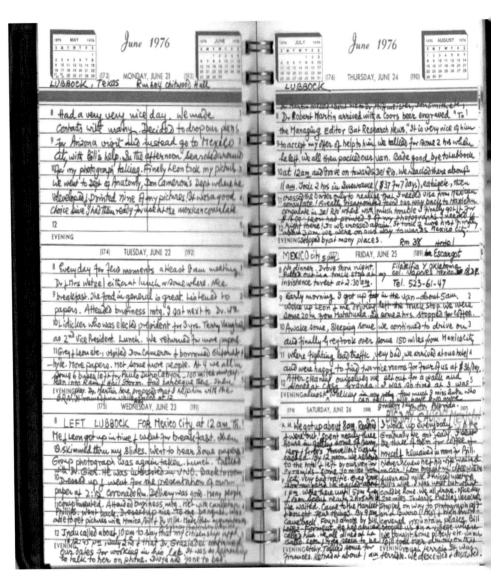

Photocopy of pages from his dairy about the trip to Mexico.

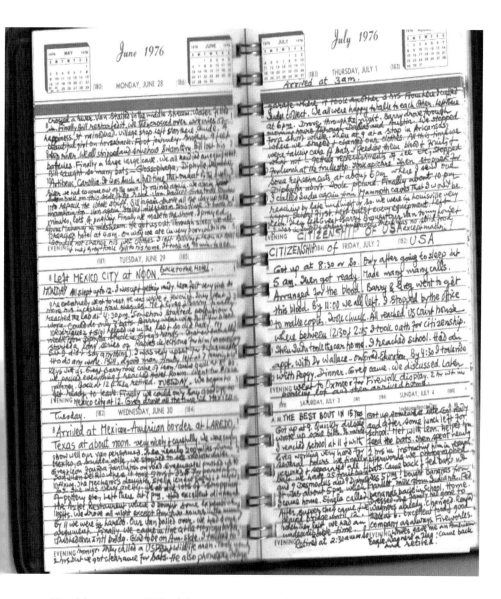

{Dad became a US citizen upon completing this journey to Mexico on July 2, 1976, and the celebration was fireworks at Oxmoor Mall in the evening.}

The day of my retirement.

A sketch drawn by Dr. KP Bhatnagar on May 29th 1961 in a letter to his wife.

Thursday, August 31, 2006

I've been at work since the morning. I did my exercises at the University Fitness Center and said goodbye to Tim Lynch and Debbie, the coaches. I told them that I would be coming, but irregularly. This afternoon, from 3–5 pm, there will be an open house reception for me, Dr. Klueber, and Dr. Wagner. Chuck Wagner is undergoing chemo and radiation therapy for lower esophageal adenocarcinoma; he will not attend the reception. The departmental faculty, students, and staff are invited, in addition to special guests specially invited by us. I will continue on this theme later today. May Guru Maharaj bless us all.

Saturday, April 26, 2014

Almost eight years have passed since I last added anything to my autobiography. Yesterday while we were at dinner with Divya and David Cantor and Jyoti and Dave Burruss, I had forgotten the word SERENDIPITY, so I asked Divya to explain what it was. She quickly spelled it out for me. I am particularly interested in this phenomenon. The Webster Dictionary defines it as a noun. [Coined by Horace Walpole (c. 1754) after his tale *The Three Princes of Serendip* (i.e., Ceylon or Sri Lanka) who made such discoveries], an apparent aptitude for making fortunate discoveries accidentally. "When I look at my list of publications, at least three serendipitous research publications light up:

(1) Skeletal muscle discovered in the pineal gland of Rhinopoma microphyllum (Journal of Anatomy). I was studying the bat pineal under an electron microscope when suddenly, a few skeletal muscle fibers came into my view. At first, they appeared to be some other organelle, but I quickly recognized them as skeletal muscle. Thus begins a scholarly paper soon to be published.

(2) A paper on parasitic nematodes (filarial) from the nasal cavity and brain of another bat species, first seen and recorded in my lab at the University of Louisville, later related observations on the brain of similar species studied at the Max Planck Institute of Brain Research, Frankfurt, Germany. This paper was published in the Trans Microscopical Society and authored by Lichtenfels, Bhatnagar, et al.

(3) My observation of a tiny VNO in Artibeus jamaicensis (Bhatnagar and Kallen, Am J Anat, 1974) led to the publication of nearly 45 papers on the vomeronasal organ (of mammals). This work is still going on.

A particular painting of three young princes going hunting is frequently found in the art world. This painting is related to the explanation of the word serendipity to convey the ability of the three princes to find an item they were not looking for. The painting has a line in one of the Arabic languages, which translates as "painted by my own hand." Sri Lanka is the region for this hunting expedition! It can be readily seen that serendipity is nowhere related to the painting and the objects therein.

Visited my autobiography on Monday, **September 14, 2015.** My cousin, Anand, is under hospice care (Riverside Hospital, California) with small cell carcinoma of the prostate. Our prayers for him **On Thursday, September 17, 2015, he passed away.** Indu, Divya, and I attended his funeral in Corona, California, on Sunday, September 27, 2015.

I am waiting for the decision on the hypophysis volumetric data on 165 species of bats (Bhatnagar, Smith, Rai, and Frahm) to be resubmitted to the Anatomical Record on August 7, 2015. I pray that it will be accepted every day, and we can move on with the rest of the work. 2015 brought me three published coauthored reports (J Morphology, Handbook of Olfaction and Taste, and Am J of Primatology). In all (without counting), I have some 145+ papers published and some 55 meeting presentations with published abstracts. The journals are peer-reviewed, and all the data on my research publications, coauthors, and affiliated institutions can be pulled out from the internet. Today (November 11) is Diwali. Our family will join us tomorrow for dinner.

Thursday, September 2, 2016

I'm just revisiting this write-up. We have just returned from the Grand European River Cruise (July 30–August 13, 2016, Viking Ingvi, Amsterdam to Budapest, with Kamla & Lal Gauri). The Hypophysis paper has been published (Anat Rec April 2016). My prayers were heard.

Thursday, November 1, 2018

Revisiting this report- I have been very sick of my back, spine, thighs, knees, legs, and occasionally feet on both sides for the last year. This excruciating pain will not let me do any walking or creative work. Since last year, I have seen two neurologists (Drs. Krystal Wilson and Young); both of these are anesthesiologists. Dr. Wilson gave me some 30 steroid injections. The last ones were in nearly the regions of L4–S3 and were part of the procedure called medial bundle branch block. These seemed to have silenced the sensory nerves. They did not. I will continue. Divya, David, Jyoti, and Dave are on the South African tour and will return home in two days.

Wednesday, August 21, 2019

Today, Indu's brother Krishna Shankar Varma is reaching India, returning from Washington, DC, after visiting his daughter Meetu, her family, and the rest of us in Louisville. I am not in good health, which prevents me from attending to my daily computer chores. After many years, I opened the internet, encouraged by my good friend Satyendra Tripathi, who asked questions about writing autobiographies. I have been a procrastinator in this respect. I started on mine sometime before my retirement (2006), and all I have produced are these 16 pages of personal history!

Dr. Divya Cantor

Distinguished people I met

A sketch drawn by Dr. KP Bhatnagar on May 29ᵗʰ 1961 in a letter to his wife.

Heinz Stephan, Heiko Frahm, Winrich Breipohl, Sir John Eccles Nobel Laureate, Dr Hirschorn, Nobel Laureate, Shriman Sardar Narasingh Rao, Maloji Rao Shitole, Jagirdar of Pohri, Shivpuri Gwalior. For a fortnight, I worked as a personal attendant to the royalty. His nephew Baba Sahib Khanvalkar, a gem of a man, took me to get Shriman's blessings. Later in Buffalo, I got to know about the suicide of Baba Sahib. He was single and had stopped taking salt. I remember his prayer before Savari, "Kuch Aisa Kardo Jaise Tum Ho, Khata Hamari Maph Karo" meaning "O Lord, do something similar to me as you are, please forgive my dashing desire." The prayer went on for a few more lines. I remember his regular visits for the Monday night service at the temple and his circ-ambulation

around the group of temples in the complex. Bade Shitole
Sahib, Shriman Narsingh Rao, would arrive with family.
His elder son Shri Krishna Rao Shitole, had arrived much
earlier in the evening; he would sit with the Dev Samiti,
especially Laxman Rao Bhonsle.

Heinz Stephan, Max-Plank-Institute of Brain
Research, Frankfurt, Germany, was a real scientist with
whom I got in touch. I began my one-year sabbatical in
Germany during Dr. Breipohl's (1978) courtesy. A year
earlier, in 1977, Dr. James B. Longley (my department
chairman at the University of Louisville Medical School)
encouraged me to visit Europe. He made it possible for me
to have everything after that casual talk in the Louisville
hallway. I applied for a sabbatical. I got it and ran with the
opportunity. Dr. Stephan was a hard worker who would
arrive at the institute at 10 a.m., avoid Frankfurt traffic, and
work all day, returning home after seven p.m.

An hour's break for coffee was taken as a ritual with
everyone in his wing. Almost every day there was a cake.
The coffee was prepared by Frau Roberg, two cups for
every person; if one was not coming, she would have been
informed. Not doing so was not good! There were no
telephone calls, incoming or outgoing, from the lab unless
necessary. One had to step out to the reception area for any
outgoing call. I was in Frankfurt on the day (in 1978) when
there was a school shooting. I was out walking after work.
Suddenly, I was stopped by two German police officers
who asked for my passport. After some broken
conversation, I was let go. Their English and my German

73

Dr. Divya Cantor

were laughable. Another such incident took place in East
Berlin. We were on a visit to Berlin, West, and East. In the
East, near the Brandenburg Gate, I went dangerously close
to East German guards, asking them, "*Wo is it Hitler's
Bunker?*". There was no reply, and my request resulted in
their conversing with each other. The few German marks
we exchanged had to be spent all there, which was spent in
a restaurant. The section of East Germany was shabby and
looked like a war zone. Back to the lab in Frankfurt, where
rigid discipline resulted in well-conceived scientific papers.
More papers were to come in the future from that
collaboration, the last being in the Anatomical Record,
2016.

This paper on the hypophysis brain data in 165
species of bats started in 1986! I accompanied Dr. Stephan
on a field trip through Thailand and India. I could fill a
whole book on my experiences. I will attempt to summarize
the trip. The paper "brain database in 165 species of bats
slowly progressed until 2016 when it was published
in *Anatomical Record*. The intervening period was some 30
years! The quality and care with which this work was
completed are exemplary. Dr. Stephan and I landed in
Bangkok and assembled our field gear, which included a
big van-like car with a driver, one scientist from the
Institute in Bangkok, and two other assistants. We paid our
respects to the Inst chief, Dr. Ratnawordhen, and took the
road towards Cheng Mai. With some local assistance, we
began to catch bats of several species. Dr. Stephan would
begin working on the previous day's catch in the morning.
The aim was to record basic data on each bat's weight, size,

74

etc., identify the species, inject freshly prepared Bouin's fluid intracardially, and leave the head in Bouins. Several days later (4 days generally), the brain was extracted by careful dissection, weighed, and other data recorded. This rigid schedule was maintained for every day that we were in Thailand. We collected a bat species in one of the caves near Chang Mai, only the fourth in number. Its brain was taken out; the rest of the bat was deposited in the Bangkok Inst's collection. Thailand is known for having as many as 120 species of bats, if not more. This was in 1986. After a rigorous collection, which included a flying squirrel, an owl, and a lot of bats, we prepared to leave for Bombay (Mumbai, India). We had to set up our mist nets in leech-infested fields, only to strip back to get rid of blood-engorged leeches, which had enough time to suck up blood.

In India, we visited Mumbai, another Gwalior collection, and then New Delhi. We collected before New Delhi in Madurai, South India.

Back in Frankfurt, I met Sir John Eccles (Nobel Laureate), who had come to the institute to meet Dr. Stephan. Dr. Heiko Frahm (my constant colleague and co-researcher) was among the other scientists we met. Once, Dr. Frahm took me to visit Heidelburg. Likewise, Dr. and Mrs. Stephan also took me to visit another castle near Frankfurt. Dr. Gerd Rehcamper (now in Düsseldorf, where the entire Stephan collection has been relocated) and a staff of seven lab tecs were among the other staff and researchers. I was invited by Prof. Winrich Breipohl to Essen, and the rest of the time in Germany was spent with him. He did his maximum to help with all phases of my research experience in Germany over so many trips to Germany (1977, 1978-79, 1986). After 1986, I visited Germany only once more, this time as a cruise passenger (with Indu and friends Drs Lal Gauri and Kamala Gauri). Germany is a country which is a must for a visit, learning or any other experience. The longest I stayed in Germany was for one year with my family, where my daughters went to school (high school) and, through hard work, achieved a great deal. Other friends were in Essen: Waldfred and Else Zinzen (our landlord), a marvelous family, our lifeline in Germany, Mrs. Liyanage, Dr. Rajiv Diddi, the late Andres Mendoza, Prof. Manfred Blank, Prof. Rolf Dermeitzel, Marian Ummels, Ferran Miragall, the Egyptian colleague working with black scorpion poison, Dr. El-Hifnawi, Lalita and Krishna Saini (a post-doc from New Delhi), On the social side, Ravi Bhatnagar was an ideal friend. He was from Gwalior, and his mother, Janak Dulari, and my family lived side by side in Gwalior.

Indu and I were invited for dinner at the Stephan residence in New Isenburg. They showed great hospitality. Dr. Stephan himself prepared the cherry dessert, lighted on the table. I was asked to sign the table cloth, which would be embroidered by Mrs. Stephan. This table cloth had the names of several Nobel Laureates and other scientists. Our auto was flat; it had to be left at the Stephan home. Dr. Frahm or some other guest took us to our residence in Frankfurt.

My family and I have been very lavishly entertained at the dinners in the homes of colleagues, at the Versailles Palace, in a castle near Essen (grants to Geran scientists were announced at that dinner, which also had no less than 50-60 courses; meats, fish, compatible wine), in Santiago-de-Compostela (magnificent seafood banquet), in Vienna (a printed dinner invitation was received from the Mayor of Vienna, Austria), and many other places.

Every place we went, we invited our colleagues for dinner. I am grateful to Indu for preparing the delicacies. Dr. Breipohl and Marian Ummels were our house guests before they spent several weeks as guests of Dr. Dan Matulionis of the Dept of Anatomy, Lexington, KY.

Our Association with Ramakrishna Vedanta Societies across the USA

In 1972, when we moved from the State University

of Buffalo, New York, to Louisville, Kentucky, we met a devoted family, Dr. Vijaya Rao and Mrs. Mukunda. They had organized a talk by Swami Adhishwarananda from New York Center. We requested Swami Bhashyananda of the Vedanta Society of Chicago to visit our society. The Swami came, and after a stay of several days and talks, he took the Louisville community under his mentorship. Some 25 devoted families, the Louisville group, began an annual summer meeting at the Ganges. Annual retreats were organized. Then followed the International Vedanta meetings.

Some ten Vedanta meetings are held yearly at the Ganges and in Chicago. Several Swamis stayed at the monastery. Some names are recorded here: Swami Bhashyananda, Swami Vardananda, Swami Kalikananda, Swami Yogeshananda, Swami Atmavratananda, Swami Atmalokananda, Swami Tapasananda, and Dr. Swami Sarveshananda. Swamis blessed the devotees: Swami Ranganathananda (Two visits), Swami Nishreyasananda, Swami Bahmroopananda, and Swamis of other orders who discoursed in Louisville. Swami Dayananda, Swami Pratygabodhanana, Swami Sumanananda (Mrs. Dr. Heera Sehra, who was ordained by Swami Dayananda, Acharya Tahal Kishore Shastri (Pranami Sampradaya), other Acharyas such as Swami Vibhudeshananada (Krishna Math), Bhai Shree Ramesh Bhai Ojha, Swami Parvati, and many other scholars have been invited for discourses, Yoga, Hindi and Hindu schools as well as other cultural sections were also opened up.

A group of devotees established a Hindu temple in Kentucky, in which I played a significant role. There was Sri Ganesh, Siva, Balaji, Radhey Krishna, Sri Ram Parivar, Ambaji, Hanumanji, Saraswati, Parvati, Kartikeya, and other deities. Each of the deities had his or her separate temple and was accessed by the priests only. All the temples were contained within a huge four-walled hall. This temple was inaugurated in 1999. Before that, in the '80s, the Ganesh murti was carved in India, brought over, and had a temporary placement in Rekha and Balaji's basement, where worship would commence. In the meantime, other murtis were carved in India, and individual temples were under construction.

The temple was established by the efforts of devotees such as Dr. Sushil Kumar, P Chandramouli and Sukanya, Mahendra and Smita Patel, Thangam Rangaswami, Dr. Udai and Chitra Kayerker, Dr. Keerthi Kemprajeurs and many other devotees and is providing a spiritual base for the Hindus in the region. Several priests headed the worship teams in the past 35 or so years. At present, Pandit Rajendra Joshi and Priest Kannan are on the worship team. Indu and I carried the ritualistic section from when we came to Louisville (1972) from Buffalo.

Through Swami Bhashyananda (Vedanta Society of Chicago), we aligned with the Chicago Center and Vivekananda Monastery and Retreat, Ganges, Michigan. For years, we have been going to the Ganges in the summer as a group. It was only in 2016 and afterward that we slowed down. I once attended an International Vedanta Retreat in the Ganges (over 25 Swamis and 700 devotees were present for three or four days). We met Swami Vidyatmananda (John R. Yale, 1913–2000, head monk, Paris, France, Ramakrishna Mission, great-grandson of Elihu Yale, who was the Governor of Madras, who for a while was strong in the slave trade, later instrumental in establishing the ivy-league Yale University in 1703. Swami Vidyatmananda authored a great book, "*A Yankee and the Swamis,*" which is highly spiritual and has real-life experiences quoted. One incident (page 169) presents remarkable evidence of how "Lord Shiva" protected a swami for all the winter months. A swami at the holy Kedarnath Temple in the Northern Himalayas. I told the Swami of my reverence for the book and him through his travelogue. In that conversation, the Swami said that he was born some 30 miles from the site where a temple and monastery were established some 60 years later, as though Thakurji (Sri Ramakrishna) had installed a caretaker Swami long before the temple and monastery became a reality. This book is a direct proof of God as Shiva. My mentor, Dr. Shyama Charan of Gwalior, India, has written a book titled "The *Origin of Kayasthas,*" which mentions the origins of Shiva, Shankar, Mahadev, Suti, Gauri, and others. It is worthwhile to study those expressions. Dr. Shymacharan says in his book that a tribe called Shankar still lives in the Karakoram mountains. Another book by the Hare Krishna Swamiji Niranjan Maharaj calls Shiva a Demi-God. I am putting this thought here because my father-in-law's middle name is Shankar! Dr. Shyamacharan's book "*The Origin of Kayasthas*" needs serious study.

❄

My Graduate Students

A sketch drawn by Dr. KP Bhatnagar in a letter written to his wife.

Of my graduate students, John Gregory Cooper took the MS degree first, then took the MD and became highly successful as a family practice physician in Cynthiana, KY. He and I published a seminal paper on the vomeronasal organ in bats (J Anatomy, 1976). Greg is an exemplary student, colleague, and physician. Greg has so much to write about the human spirit that it is impossible to write about what he is. Maybe I will return to him again.

Barry Spoonamore was an equally hard-working graduate. He did a project on the AV-node in *Eptesicus fuscus* (Acta Anat 1979). After taking the MS, he went on to get his MD and is a well-recognized physician in Danville, KY.

RC Kennedy completed the MS project (Anat Rec 1987) on the Quantitative Studies on the Human Olfactory

Bulb, getting his MD later. Leon Kundrotus also took MS and MD degrees. Some years ago, he wrote to me as Col. Leon Kundrotus, a superfine member of the US Air Force. He specialized in gastroenterology.

There have been other MS, MD, and Ph.D. students, both here in the US and abroad, for which I was a mentor and thesis examiner.

In India, the name of Dr. Shiv Sahai Saxena, who had asked me five years before I got my M.Sc (Zoology) degree to work and obtain a Master's degree remains. I worked hard under his direction and became the first student of a newly established university, the Vikram University, in the ancient city of Avantika, or Ujjain also called the city of Mahakal or the city of King Vikramaditya. Dr. Shyama Charan Shrivastava took a special interest in me. He felt I should study abroad and introduced me to Professor Dr. William Abel Wimsatt at Cornell University, Ithaca, New York. His graduate students' quota being full, he sent me off to his student, Professor Dr. Frank Clements Kallen, at the State University of New York at Buffalo, where I began my graduate study in Anatomy with thesis work on "*Olfaction in Bats.*" In January 1967, when I arrived in Buffalo in knee-deep snow, I was prepared to fight the weather, and I did. I signed up for a course in physiology (Dr. Bishop) in which I did not do well; for a while, I was reading the book, but the exam came from the instructor's lectures, and I did not know that. I was unaware of this technicality; I was still carrying the notion that I was an Associate Professor of Zoology in India and therefore knew much already. Struggling hard, I stepped into the first full semester with Anatomy courses, which I handled with grace and high performance. Then followed short but highly research-oriented courses.

Buffalo had a tradition for every Ph.D. scholar to take at least one course from every faculty member before taking the prelims. I satisfied every requirement. A day came when Dr. Kallen came into my room and said, "Kunwar, now you can call your family. We will keep you." I sent the good news to Indu, whose papers were ready. Divya wrote back, "Daddy, we are coming." So, on June 18, 1968, Indu, Divya, and Jyoti flew Pan American Airlines to Buffalo, New York, via Kennedy Airport, where a friend saw their direction to Buffalo. Dr. Kallen was ready with a huge bouquet of red roses. He and I received my family. The house at 270 Langfield Drive was set. Mrs. Ram B Ram cooked meals for us and our days began. Divya and Jyoti were admitted to schools. Our house was some 2 miles from the school. I never took the bus to school, saving fifty cents on the fare per trip. Sometimes I would buy the chocolate-covered long biscuit, the same thing I would buy in Frankfurt, Germany! These were for Indu.

Shri Har Kishore Bhatnagar helped me with my admission to first-year college in 1952. He was a professor of physics. My Zoology faculty for M.Sc were: Dr. SS Saxena, Dr. SC Shrivastava, KS Kulshreshtha, Saxena, Gyan Prakash Asthana, HC Agrawal, Gaur, Chaturvedi. At the end of my B.Sc, we compiled a yearbook sort of named *Upasana*. I was the editor. Instead of printing (there were no funds), I hand-wrote all submissions in whatever language the submissions came in. Dr. Chand Narayan Haksar (Chemistry) is in the group photo. Prof. Agarkar was the top educator in Botany. My fellow students were VC Gupta, HJ Asati, CL Bhasin, Surendra Bhatnagar (son of Bal Swaroop Bhatnagar), and Suri.

Shri Harish Chandra, the Central Library Librarian, became my savior. He appointed me as a library clerk with a salary scale of Rupees 40-3-70 plus an allowance of nearly the same value as my salary. My best friends in the library were Malhar Narayan Dharkar, Makhan Lal Ojha, Ram Charan Lal Savita, Narayan Prasad Mudgal, Ganesh Vishnu Gore, his peon Kalla, and Moti Ram. The head librarian was Chandrika Prasad Mishra, who supported me in going to college for five consecutive years. The head clerk was Sapre. The Head librarian was replaced by V S Moghe, who too let me go to college, but early on, the Dy Director of Education, Mr. ..., refused to support me; either going to college or working in the library! Another educational, Babu Lal, helped me to continue college, so it was against so many odds that I could continue college. My routine was to get up early in the morning, sometimes taking a walk to the peak of Hanuman Tekri, which was seen behind our house in Lashkar-Gwalior, then reach the library before 7:30 am, and leave after 10 am direct to the college. In between, one of my brothers will bring me lunch from home. From 10:30 to 4:30 pm, I attend college, return to the library, work until 7:30 pm, return home, have a meal, make light prep for the next day, then go to bed.

After clearing the B.Sc, I began the rigorous joint study with Gopal Singh Dogra (later Dr. Dogra Ph.D., University of Lucknow) at his house, so after the evening meals, I would rest a bit, then bicycle down to the Dogra residence in Kampoo (the big house of Major Kartar Singh, Gopal'sGopal's father). I slept until 1:30 am, studied until 6:30 am, reached my home, and before 7:30 am, I was back in the library for the next full day to begin. This is how the two years for the M.Sc were conducted. This routine earned me a First Class First Honor. Subsequent rewards all depended on my achievement in M.Sc.

Soon after the M.Sc, to my disappointment, I was appointed as a lecturer in Zoology at Hamidia Inter College, Bhopal, famous for its undisciplined students who would do all but study. Somehow, I was carrying on. On the 44th day of my stay at Bhopal, I now do not remember how I went to the Education Secretariate seeking to meet Mr. Chaturvedi IAS, the Education Secretary. He assured me that I should be patient and stay in the post. After this meeting, I again said hello to him in the market. Immediately after that, my transfer to the College of Science, Raipur, was affected. This was a postgraduate college. I met many scholars here, such as Dr. Karam Singh (Principal), Dr. RN Singh (head, Zoology Dept), Dr. Sharma, Mr. JN Saxena, Ms. Saraswati Sivram Iyer, and Prof. Raj Krishna Khanna, with whom I produced an abstract for the Indian Science Congress. Khanna was a very good friend, and he came to Raipur on a transfer from Bhopal (from Dr. Ravi Mathur'sMathur's department). I missed him at Indore. This abstract was on the AV node of the escrow. Mrs. Iyer, IP Tiwari, and attendant Yadu (who remembered me by name when I visited the college after I had gone on to America).

I had some good students, such as SL Das. Five of the young lecturers were given apartments. These were Datta (Physics), PC Mishra (Physics), Mahesh Chandra Saxena (Botany), myself, and two others. We employed a cook from Rewa, who gave us three good meals daily. He had a day off once a week. This apartment was opposite the Zoology Department, making it very convenient for me. In the main market, there was the Dudhadariya Vaishnav Temple, which I visited every Tuesday evening and was blessed by the Mahanta Maharaj. Generally, I attended the Arati. I stayed for two years in Raipur. It was here that my marriage proposal came from Jammu & Kashmir, from Mr. BS Varma. Here was my destiny to be engaged to Indu. In 1960 I was transferred to another postgraduate college, Holkar College, Indore, for one year, and was transferred again as Assistant Professor, Degree College, Jhabua. After a year, he again transferred to Guna. The name Guna sounds like many bells ringing at the same time. As mentioned earlier, I would have liked certain things to happen to me (such as the dream of Divya and Jyoti being born several days ahead of their actual birth, the room number, and the exact words from my lecture at Raipur). Guna falls on the Gwalior-Guna-Bhopal-Indore bus route. The entrance into Guna was so majestic, a tree-lined avenue, that I wished I lived in Guna each time I took that route passing through. My wish came true, and I transferred to Guna for the maximum period there (1962, January-

1967, till I left for Buffalo, New York). Such things were my strong convictions.

Dr. Divya Cantor

A brief calendar of my life span

A sketch drawn by Dr. KP Bhatnagar in a letter written to his wife.

On March 21, 1934, I was born in Gwalior. I remember many scenes as a toddler, such as: swinging in a cradle; insisting on a certain type of long cloth (dhoti, which my mother tailored to suit my leg-length); taking a fancy to eat "Laddus" (dessert); walking with my grandfather, who freely gave me candies; a visit to a family friend's house at Moti Jheel (a water station some 10 miles away from our home); riding in a horse-driven carriage (called a tonga), a form of hospitality offered to both of us (my grandfather and I); my pre-kindergarten attendance; admission to Grade 1 (it was difficult to take me away from home; upon reaching Gorki School, I refused to enter the class; my grandpa bribed me by making me sit on the threshold while he bought me either Peda or Jalebees). That piece of stone on which I sat is still there. I like to visit there when I can. Gorkhi School was a palace donated to be a prominent school for grades 1 to 8. I remember the great rooms, stairs, the principal's (Pradumna Kumar Srivastava, who would always walk with an umbrella in hand and just that to punish rowdy young ones) chambers, a huge well, several large compounds, Kamrakh compound, large fields for the drill by the red-socked stern drill instructor, and several trees with various fruits coming on seasonally, such as mulberry (Shahtoot). Our math teacher was Mr. Nashikkar, whose house we passed on the way to school. I can draw the route, which had large homes. One or two small temples, a Bhatnagar family house where one of the five brothers had been married five times! He was known to be a rough guy. I have noticed a Temple at the bend, at many turns where the road makes a loop. The Gorkhi school was within the boundaries of the former palace.

I remember the birth of the son of Madhav Rao Scindia (the son of the ruler Jiwaji Rao Scindia). That whole week, desserts were prepared and distributed several pounds to everyone round the clock. No one may have been spared from receiving the sweet gifts. The central attraction in Lashkar (add Gwalior and Morar to make Greater Gwalior) is Maharaj Bada, which had (and still has) Palatal statues, Victoria Market, a post office building, Regal Cinema Hall, a bandstand, the Statue of Madhav Rao Scindia (JM Sciendia's father, the former ruler), Krishna Ram Baldev Bank, Sarafa Bazar, Alijah Durbar Press (the Gwalior Gazette was printed there, in which my appointment as lecturer in Zoology was published. And there were temples on every bend. Every Sunday, a band played tunes from the bandstand. My brothers and I were always in attendance. I have always liked bands.

Let's get back to more experiences from the Gorkhi middle school, where I passed out with a diploma (passed Middle School). This was the first door for further academia and one at which quite a few stopped and managed their family business. The school would supply delicious cooked black garbanzos for lunch. I remember my physics classes; students were punished in class for not doing their homework.

I entered VC High School (Victoria Collegiate High School, grades 9 and 10) from middle school. I passed these classes and declared no more education for myself, which was okay with my father, but not with my mother, who had me admitted to one intermediate college, Jayendraganj, in the Science Math group, which did not suit me at all. I lost two years in this trial. I remained unsuccessful. My mother also took me to Prof. Har Kishore Bhatnagar (Physics), a relative. He recommended my admission to the Principal, Dr. Shiv Sahai Saxena. This was 1952. Before this, I passed the matriculation exam (10th grade, 1949). In 1956, a B.Sc (Bachelor's Degree) was achieved, and in 1958, a Master of Science in Zoology was awarded by Vikram University. An appointment in the teaching faculty follows. Thus, I taught for eight years in the Madhya Pradesh Educational System (1958–66); on January 6, 1967, I left Westward for America. These eight years were the golden years for me.

I had bright students everywhere I went; we quickly spotted each other. Some memorable students were SL Das in Raipur, P Bhojwani; Nirmal Bhatnagar; Prof. Gogate; and a rental room in the residence of Sri Rajendra Saxena (the income tax officer). This house was in Radio Colony and towards my college, where I used to cycle daily. I would buy two eggs and make a delicious omelet after returning from school. Come dinner time, I would bicycle to a Gujarati restaurant, later moving to a restaurant that recently opened a few houses away from my room. The Rajendra Saxena family was an ideal family of four (Rajendra, Saroj, Kiran, and Renu) with whom I remained in contact for many years after I moved to America. Somehow, the Saxena family could not come to the Delhi railway station while my Barat was returning from Dehradun (April 29, 1961). Indu never met this family because I was transferred to Jhabua immediately after marriage. The Principal, Dr. Bhagwat, of Holkar College, Indore, let me off several weeks earlier to partake in my own marriage. I wish there was a teaching methods course in every department to teach the particular course. That was not the case; still, there may not be any such facility.

We lived in Jhabua for one year. Chanda enrolled in college, and Kishan returned to Gwalior. My mother set up our house and returned to Gwalior also. We rented a small two-room house from Seth on the main street. There was no water system. Every morning, Meghnad, the peon, would arrive early and fetch water from the tap one floor down. Some familiar names from the group of colleagues were Mr. Vajpai (the principal), Kelkar (Chemistry), KC Jain (Economics), Khare (Hindi), and Khera (later moved to England), and another lecturer came to Zoology while I was on transfer to Guna. Here, I set up little research on the bacula of some Indian Megachiroptera. This short paper was published in 1967 in J Mammalogy.

Mr. BS Varma sent me four preserved *Cynopterus*. One day it was very rainy and windy. In the morning, while walking to college, I saw a big tree branch had broken, lots of *"Pteropus"* were dead and injured, and their babies were crying. I collected seventeen bats, put away one injured tortoise, and carried them to school. Over the day, I preserved these bats. They may still be in the collection of the Jhabua Department. These fruit bats are large, *Pteropus giganteus*, which are extremely difficult to capture. In Gwalior, I shot them. In Thailand, Dr. Stephan collected a few by tying a net to two poles and letting the tree-dwelling bats fly through the net with the help of the Randive (educationist) and Shrivastava (attorney) families; we later made friends with them. There were two Temples for Indu and me to offer our prayers. Langur monkeys (*Presbylatus entalus),* the black-faced, long-tailed monkeys, were hopping and stealing food items. Indu lost the bread dough a few times. I am reminded of the Hanuman Temple in

Shimla near the main market. The monkeys there are intelligent. They do not steal from the ingoing devotees nor attack the shop keepers who display their wares, including food items. Still, they follow the returning pilgrims from whom they will snap food and personal items such as eyeglasses, purses, wallets, etc. After snapping, they run and sit on any nearby tree; one packet of food will not satisfy them; at least three are to be thrown at them. Only then will they return the objects taken. In my group, my brother-in-law and sister-in-law were robbed by these monkeys who held Shobha, who stood with her hands raised praying, with the monkey unzipping her pockets, pulling peanuts and other items. Krishna, the brother-in-law's eyeglasses, were taken away and returned in mutilated shape for three packets of food items bought and thrown away.

We had such incidents in a Florida animal park and elsewhere. There are examples wherever monkey groups live in the open. I saw a video in a viral email where a swami delivered a religious discourse. A "Langur" walks up to the Swami and places his hand over the Swami's head, likely blessing the Swami. I could not tell if this video was doctored. In Rajasthan state in India, there is a temple of rats where numerous rats are running around. The pilgrims have to step in with caution.

From Jhabua, I came with Indu this time to Guna, where I always wanted to be with good faculty, colleagues, and students. I stayed here from 1962-66; Divya and Jyoti were conceived (1962, 1964) here but born at Gwalior hospital (Dr. Ollei, MD); I enrolled in the National Cadet Corp (NCC) as a Lieutenant and got trained at Kamtee (near Nagpur) and Purandhar (Poona); being a senior commander, I looked over eight companies of 200 cadets. We received Brigadier Randhawa (the National NCC Commander) on several occasions. Lt. General Pindaley, returning from the Gaza Strip as commander, was driving through Guna to Mhow to take over the Mhow Cantonment. For his one-day stay in Guna, I took care of the hospitality. Dinner and breakfast (5 a.m.) were served. The General promptly arrived at our residence (Mathur Bldg, Guna) at 5 p.m. He sent me a copy of his letter to Brig Randhawa on the cadre of officers under his command! The able students in my alfa company were Shinde, Sardar Rajender Singh, Tufail Ahmad Lucknawi, Kabul Chand Jain, Aruna Agarkar, Mr. Gupta (the high school biology teacher), Chandra Roop Singh, Prem Sharma, and Prof. RP Gupta (Physics); the sweetshop making son papdi, the bus stand, and the temple again before entering Guna, traveling South. At Bina railway station, I received Prof. Ralph Martin Wetzel (on field collection through India). He got my contact through membership in the Mammalogical Society. I took him to Guna. He stayed at the Circuit House, a few hundred meters from our home. I took him to my Dept. Gopi Lal, the Asst, was always with us. Gopi was a marvelous person. Away from college, he worked at home helping Indu. Dr. Wetzel (University of Connecticut, Storrs) became a good friend, and it was he who met me at New York Kennedy Airport and invited me to stay with them for a few days.

He had a graduate student, Sana Atallah (perhaps from Jordan). While driving to Wetzel's home, I asked him the first question: "Why are these cars signaling right or left?" The answer was easy. From Guna, Dr. Wetzel, Gopi, and I went to Chanderi and collected bats from the "Khooni Darwaza (bloody gate)." One night we stayed in Chanderi. Indu had packed breakfast. Dr. Wetzel left for Hyderabad to instruct in the field course in mammalogy. We arranged for a live specimen of pangolin, the ant-eater. Tufail Ahmad Lucknawi was from Chanderi and also a faithful biology student.

Mr. Deole, a good friend and NCC officer, was an economics lecturer. Dr. Pendse (who spoke very loudly) was the principal. Dr. Kaveeshwar and Mr. Kataria were principals in their own right. Kataria was ruthless but treated me nicely.

I spent a few days in Storrs and flew to Buffalo, where I was received by Dr. Frank Clements Kallen (Ph.D. Cornell, flew missions in the Korean War), a chain smoker and a thorough gentleman, proficient in German, French, and perhaps Polish languages. In the lab, Esther Desenroth had a daughter, Judy, and a mother. Prof. OP Jones (hematology, EM) was the chair. Later, Harold Brody replaced him. Other professors were Joseph C. Lee, Richard H. Weber, E. R. Hayes, Chat Glomski, Vijay Shankar, Rolf Flygare, Richard Webster, Roger Ferguson, Frances Sansone, and staff: Helen, Evelyn, Katarina, Rosemary Gagliardi, Mary Boerst, James Kokoros, and

John Wirth (EM). Kallen was researching with Carl Gans (later to become editor of J Morphology) and Clyde F. Herried. After receiving his Ph.D., Father Joe Tomasulo returned to society, and Richard M. Webster became a minister! He sent me a book as a gift, which I could use. I have been able to recall nearly all of the people in the Department at Buffalo with whom I spent time from January 1967 through April 1972 when we joined the Anatomy Department at Louisville. In March of 1972, I was away from my lab. A distinguished gentleman came looking for me and waited. He was Professor James Bain Longley, chairman of the Dept of Anatomy at Louisville, who was out driving through places with recruitable Ph.D.'s for his department. He sort of interviewed me for over two hours.

The afternoon was very rainy. I invited Professor James Bain Longley for tea at my residence. He accepted. We drove to my home. He met Indu, Divya, and Jyoti. After a good visit, we returned to the parking lot. He forgot in which lot his car was parked, for Capen Hall was surrounded by lots in every direction. Eventually, he saw the car and said goodbye, leaving for the next destination. Such was his determination. Within days, I was invited to Louisville. He received me at the terminal and drove to Bowman Field restaurant, Ho Cow, for lunch. He gave me my appointment with the words "Kunwar, read and sign the contract if acceptable." I signed the next day after I checked with Dr. Kallen. Then I met the faculty and gave a presentation. I stayed with him for a day, and he showed what kind of scholar-scientist man he was on numerous occasions. The Cambridge-educated editor of Stain Technology with an open-door policy was the person who encouraged me to go to Europe. At that time, I had three and a half (a short paper in *Experientia).* I was recommended for my promotion to Associate Professor with tenure. I had no idea what tenure was. Having gone through the process without the risks, I made it through, fortunately.

Otherwise, it was a dangerous step to be so early! I traveled to Paris to attend the International Physiological Meeting, presenting my work on the nasal anatomy of bats. There, attending the banquet at Versailles Palace, the seating began at 8 p.m. with the grand banquet ending after midnight; I was sort of sleepy over eight courses of dinner with an equal number of wines to enjoy. From Paris to Frankfurt, Germany, for a seminar with the Heinz Stephan group at the Max-Planck Institute for Brain Research, arranged by Winrich Breipol of Essen, then flew to New Delhi, India, for a visit of a week or so, before returning home. In 1986, I made several trips to Germany. The last trip was to Frankfurt-Thailand-India with Dr. Stephan. It is under lots of poor health, pain, and stress that I am typing this auto in a free manner. I have difficulties due to my eyes being inflamed, back pain (spinal stenosis, perianal pain, am on antibiotics, Tramadol and Tylenol as pain killers), heart medications (Bystolic, Lisinopril, Amlodipine), several anti-constipation medicines (Mira-Lax, Metamucil, senna*, Kaya*m, Phillips milk of magnesium), many vitamins (multivitamins, protein. white powder, green powder) and several other OTC medicines.

Divya is filling my medicine tubes for one week at a time. Jyoti calls every day at about 8 a.m., followed by Divya. Indu does all my work to feed us; shopping outings, maintenance on the house, and social obligations. Several friends are sick. Besides me, Dr. Lal Gauri, Satish Chandra, Kiran Shah, Dr. Baby Jose, Dr. Kailash Sabharwal, and others. Some friends have passed away (Dr. Pran Ravani, Dr. Thangam Rangaswami, Dr. Subhash Lonial).

     I never imagined that I would be this handicapped. The first words to Indu I spoke were the next day after marriage and after the lunch that we would depart for Gwalior by the evening train. Indu seemed to be pleased to hear that. All the Baraat was accommodated in one compartment. Indu was given a section of it, and my brothers took good care of her. I joined her later and was pleased to converse with her. At Gwalior, she was given a separate patore; she never complained about anything and was very compatible with my mother, respecting her in all possible ways. After a while, Krishna came to fetch her back to Dehradun. I did not take the separation even for those few weeks well. She returned after attending a wedding in Agra. Then, a few weeks later, I went to Dehradun, where I stayed for a week, visiting sight-seeing places, such as FRI, Sulphur Springs, and Mussorie. We did not go and see the pass out. Happily, Indu and I returned to Gwalior. Then, a huge rain storm poured upon us, spoiling our clothes. After that, Indu and I returned to Gwalior. I enjoyed the beautiful city.

The Marriage of Science and Spice

My principal, Dr. Bhagwat, and chair, Prof. Gogate, was gracious enough to give me an extra week off. Mrs. Saroj Varma and her family could never meet Indu. We reached Jhabua straight from Gwalior without stopping at Indore and took a train from Gwalior-Bhopal-Ratlam to Jhabua. I had a good time at Jhabua. My mother and brother, Kishan, returned to Gwalior, while Chanda stayed with us and attended college. As Mr. Maru, a Professor of English was a top bridge player, I began my research with the baculum of bats using sunlight as a source for clearing the specimens. Those cleared tissues are in the custody of Dr. Tim D. Smith at Slippery Rock University. Once or twice, I visited Dr. Sharma, who was stationed at Indore, or Bhopal. I was visiting about my foreign leave. One under-secretary helped me a lot.

Then I was transferred again to Guna, my favorite place. I made many good friends among students and faculty, the general public, and residents from all walks of life. Some names come to memory: Mr. Mathur (the contractor), his brother-in-law Mr. RamGopal Mathur, masterji, Bhuaji, Prof Gholap, Prof Dole, Kunwar Chandra Bhan Singh of Garha, Guna, my lab assistant Gopilal, and Mr. Karnadhar. Guna had several NCC companies. I was the senior commander. I used to command the ceremonial parade of over a thousand NCC cadets, giving a salute to the attending dignitaries. That was some show of planning. I arranged an NCC camp with Brig Randhawa at Guna. Hospitality was organized for Brigerdiar Indaley, who was returning as a commander of the Gaza Strip. I received Prof. Ralph Maartin Wetzel (Univ of Connecticut, Storrs, the USA, arranged by myself). I made several bat-collecting trips to Garha Castle, Bajrangarh Fort, and the Temple of Devi, who looked at you in every corner of the sanctuary. This fort was only 20 miles or so, a biking distance. Other friendly companies were Kabool Chand Jain, Shinde, Cadet Singh, and Mr. Gupta, a high school biology teacher who was a family friend.

In a nutshell, Guna was heavenly, where gems like Divya and Jyoti were conceived and brought glory to their family. In Guna, I was admitted to the State University of New York at Buffalo under Dr. Kallen and maintained my graduate status, eventually earning my Doctor of Philosophy in Anatomy (1972). In the same year, before the degree was awarded, I was appointed Assistant Professor of Anatomy at the University of Louisville School of Medicine.

In 1978, I received my tenure and promotion to Associate Professor of Anatomical Sciences and Neurobiology, went to Germany for one year's sabbatical leave, attended an International Symposium on Bat Research, and received Swami Ranganathananda (to become the president, Maharaj of Belur Math, Kolkata, India) as our house guest while I was away to New Mexico attending the International Symposium in New Mexico. Indu and my children were the lucky hosts to receive the personal blessings of the Swami. Thus, 1978 was one of the most blessed years, filled with multiple activities and life-changing events for my family and me. The great Swami visited Louisville one more time. In 1984, I was promoted to full professor.

During my teaching period, I first taught Dental Anatomy, later Human Embryology, and Gross Anatomy for the medical class for over 30 years. I retired in 2006.

Tuesday, October 22, 2019

During this period, I have published over 153 peer-reviewed scientific papers and am still counting. A summary follows.

Earlier, I have narrated the publication of three papers (Turtox New, Current Science, India, and J Mammalogy, USA). The paper on the abnormal genital system of the leech received a reprint request from Cambridge University, UK. Dr. JB Longley was the chair until 1986, when he retired, and Dr. Fred Roisen came as chair of anatomy. That was the same year I went on my second sabbatical. A third sabbatical was granted to me, but I did not avail of it.

For my Ph.D. research, I selected two bat species: one *Artibeus jamaicensi*s, sent by Dr. William Wimsatt of Cornell University, and brought over from Mexico by William Lopez Foment, and kept alive by me at Buffalo for several years; One of the chapters in my dissertation was on the histomorphology of the nasal chamber. I described a pin-size sensory organ – the VOMERONASAL ORGAN. It was briefly described, neurons were counted, and a new structure was introduced—the para-vomeronasal ganglion in bats. I have not counted how many papers I have published on the VNO of different vertebrates, including humans. I will not be surprised if this number adds up to 50 or even more.

My co-researcher in this research was Dr. Timothy DuWolf Smith, born in 1966. I was born in 1934. While here in Louisville in 1998 or so, Tim wrote to me, and as a result of that correspondence, we published our first joint paper in the *Journal of Anatomy* (2000). After that, continuous papers have been published to this date.

We have shown that humans DO NOT possess a VNO beyond six months of fetal life. It appears in the human fetus by day 42 or so, begins to disappear soon, and by six months in the uterus, there is hardly a cartilaginous vestige remaining. There is no VNO sensory neuroepithelium remaining. For the last 300 years, hundreds of morpho-functional reports on adult human VNO have been published with all sorts of associated functions. We call it research on a phantom organ.

Since our reports relating to the human VNO, there has been a lull in producing such imaginative research. Otherwise, there is evidence of several papers on the human VNO per year in the literature. Since old-world primates and Megachiroptera (fruit bats) do not have a VNO, reptiles (snakes and other mammals) and most other mammals (excluding non-human primates and fruit bats) are devoid of a VNO. The fact that humans are endowed with a VNO only during the fetal period (approximate days 42–180) might have confused the issue. In humans and in all those groups where a VNO is devoid, you would have to explain the developmental reasoning behind reporting the presence or absence of a VNO. This also means no practical conclusions can be drawn from missing neural tissue (neural VNO epithelium). On the other hand, where there is a neuroepithelial tube, VN nerves, and an accessory olfactory bulb, the organ is functional and serves as an ORGAN OF ACCESSORY OLFACTION wherever it occurs. Snakes have the best development of a VNO.

❄

Dr. Divya Cantor

Our best pieces of research

A sketch drawn by Dr. KP Bhatnagar on May 15th 1961 in a letter written to his wife.

1. Settling the controversy regarding the human VNO, a 300-year-old debate
2. Morphology of 165 species of the bat hypophysis
3. Morphology of the pineal gland of bats
4. Several reports on the serendipitous topics
5. Reports on gross human anomalies

I cannot find a research report which is not original and which may be classified as of no or little value.

To give some examples of serendipitous
findings: Observation of parasitic filiarioid nematodes embedded in the olfactory epithelium and other olfactory tissues, including the brain of Tadarida Mexicana in the serial series of the nasal region, then finding similar forms in the brain ventricular systems of the same species in the Max-Planck, Frankfurt collection of similar species Further research brought out the conclusion that these were parasitic filiaroids which entered the nose of these ground-feeding bats through the olfactory epithelium, eventually reaching the ventricular brain system (Trans Microsc Socy, 1981); Patching of the brain of Desmpodus has been observed (unpublished; see Desmodus atlas).

I have a few other serendipitous reports published in my scientific life. The scientific debate on the human VNO controversy (still not settled in the minds of researchers) can be added to this list.

The finding of a VNO in my Ph.D. research on Artibeus and Myotis (lack of the VNO) and the subsequent explosion of all those VNO studies in 50 years in humans,

105

primates, rodents, and other animals can also be considered serendipitous.

Interesting enough, the following questions (without answers) continue to exist on the VNO:

- Why is the VNO found only in Amphibia, Reptilia, and Mammalia vertebrates?
- In every group, there are a few species lacking the VNO. Why so?
- The explanation for the lack of a VNO in non-human primates and the megachiropteran fruit bats. What might be the function of a VNO? Whatever the function is, it should be uniformly similar in all species where it is present, not have so many different functions assigned to the organ in various species.
- The relationship between the olfactory tissues and accessory olfactory tissues.

These and other related questions await serious, in-depth attention.

❄

Friends

A sketch drawn by Dr. KP Bhatnagar on May 15th 1961 in a letter written to his wife.

Mahendra Nath Saxena aka Rajjan

My middle and high school friend, and a member of Dev Samiti, Kaila Maharani, and Kunwar Maharaj Temple, Gwalior. He was the son of Madho Singh, a Magistrate who lived close to us with his parents and family. We used to cycle to Victoria Collegiate High School. He would drive the bicycle while I took the rear seat. One day, we went up the hill named "A Kothi, a mansion" with Balwant Rao Bhaiya. He got angry over something and rolled down the hill, leaving me behind on the hilltop to walk the miles back to the plains. I did not argue with a very well-built and

107

muscular young man. His progress in school was not good. His father had him admitted to a school in Solan, Punjab, where he used to write sentimental letters to me. Eventually, one day, he disappeared, never to be seen again. So, this is the story of my best friend.

Kripa Sharan Saxena, Divisional Forest Officer, M Pradesh (retired)

I met KS, as I called him, for the first time in Vidisha (near Bhopal) at the home of my maternal cousin, Dr. Om Prakash Bhatnagar (deceased). He knew that I was appointed as a lecturer of Zoology at the "notorious" Hamidia Intermediate College, Bhopal, KS, and offered me his rental room close to walking distance to my college. My 44-day stay in Bhopal and subsequent transfer to the College of Science Raipur are detailed elsewhere in my autobiography. I was eating out in the market and remembered the homeowners from the two beautiful girls they had. But this note is about KS. Maybe he came for one day and stayed during his official travels. We met three years later when he was also transferred to Jhabua; I was moving from Indore to Jhabua. After a year, I again moved to Guna, my favorite place, for four years. After having a wonderful time there in January 1967, I was flying Pan American One to Buffalo, New York, with a see-off one would not imagine, for I published two scientific papers, trained NCC cadet companies, made friends for life, and Mr. Katare, the harshest principal known, garlanding me at my farewell.

Once, when I went with him to his forest lodge in Jhabua, his attendant prepared the dinners so slowly that it took many minutes for the roti to be baked, but despite the delay, I remember the meals being delicious.

Dr. Gopal Singh Dogra, Ph.D.

At the M.Sc first year level (1956–57), we had 16 students and a full vibrating class. When the finals came, 13 of those failed. Satyendra Dutt Tripathi and I advanced to M. Sc II, with S. Dutt focusing on fishes and Gopal on entomology. I have always had a strong interest in taxonomy as a whole. Here too, I had memorized the entire classification of INSETA down to the level of every subfamily, with at least two Latin names for each related species. Our Entomology textbook was by Imms of a British University. I remember congratulating him on his award by the Royal Society of England (FRS). He responded immediately, too, by penning a few lines in his handwriting that read, "I hope that you have excellent students." How important that sentiment is. Yes, sir, I did have excellent students everywhere I went, and most of them kept in touch with me. There are many examples of excellent students who received the Nobel prize, with their students receiving the same coveted award. Professor J Z Young is well-known for not receiving the Nobel Prize with nine of his students! Many fathers and Nobel laureate sons are known in the annals of the Nobel award.

Both Satyendra and I were working at the same time. We were going to school (1952–58 B.Sc and M.Sc) and were tired since we had to study at night. Once in Dr. SCS's lecture, I was napping, at which Gopal was elbowing me to wake up, at which Dr. SCS chided him, "Why did he wake me up?" It has been my style to select a scholar student and jointly execute our studies. The culminating point came at the M.Sc level, where Gopal and I were studying together, waking up at 1:30 am and studying till 6:30 am. Daily breakfast at Gopal's nearby, adjoining his parental home. This rigorous exercise earned me a First Class First in Zoology from Vikram University, Ujjain, India. Gopal, still very young, was the Dean of Agriculture at Solan University, Punjab. He talked to his daughter on the telephone when he slumped to his passing away. He had a heart condition. A good friend and a scholar were taken from our hands.

Dr. Satyendra Dutt Tripathi

A dear family friend since 1956, we have been in close touch with each other. The above paragraph narrates some of the golden qualities of Satyendra. At the M.Sc final (1958), the three of us had some identical qualities. In addition to visiting the USA, Canada, Germany, and other countries, peer-reviewed publications in top scientific journals, Gopal was an athletic sportsman. Satyendra (MA, English, M.Sc Zoology, Ph.D., has an excellent command of English as the language), (Director of Fisheries, Indian Government), Gopal went to Munich, Germany, for two years to research honey bees. It was sad that he never came to Louisville, whereas Satyendra visited me on two occasions, staying a few days. In 1958, while on my way to attend my convocation to receive my M.Sc diploma (Pandit Nehru was the chief guest for the occasion), I was his house guest, meeting his parents and family. Satyendra's father was the former teacher of the Maharaja of Narsinghgarh. I was taken to the palace to tour the fort and Palace Narasinghgarh.

Dangerous Animals Handled

A sketch drawn by Dr. KP Bhatnagar on May 23rd 1961 in a letter written to his wife.

A quick patting of the rump of an Indian tigress at dinner across a wire mesh at Shivpuri National Park. The tigress had not been fed for a whole day; she did not care for the pat! Next come three full-grown Indian cobras (Naja tripudia). One, as in the Gwalior Fort, a snake charmer played by putting the cobra in my neck. I did not enquire whether the cobra had extracted fangs. The other two cobras were wild and had fully developed venom glands. One of these was contained in a glass container. It was

112

resting on the divider wall between the bathroom and toilet; both were occupied at the time! The third cobra was caught from a well in the wild where it seemed to have fallen into the well. Gopal and I had hot ropes, a mud pot (cracked for water to fill the pot), and a mud cover. The pot was lowered into the well, guided by the ropes, the snake was coaxed into the pot, the cap closed the mud pot, and the pot was gently pulled up. Keeping the pot on the bicycle handle, we returned home to our study room. The snake was chloroformed and transferred to a glass container in a listless condition. The next day, it was moved to school and dissected for its venom apparatus; the venom gland was loaded to capacity. In the same field where we caught the cobra from the well, Gopal uncovered a viper (another deadly poisonous snake) and ran after the swiftly moving snake, which escaped. Our actions were foolish, but they were daring at the time!

On another occasion, as we proceeded for a short pilgrimage, we stopped at a waterfall at Bhadavana (near Utila, Morar, and Gwalior) for bathing. Within moments of our party entering the fall, a stream of snakes was coming through the fall. I did not wait to identify the species!

There have been many incidences of lurking danger while collecting bats from caves, homes, and places where bats could hide. I even requested my father-in-law to get some preserved bats from Jammu (Regional Research Lab, Jammu, and Kashmir) for my research at Jhabua. He obliged, and the research was completed and published (J Mammalogy, 1967).

As part of a wedding party, we were out to tour the Kaziranga National Park near Guwahati, Assam, India. Four of us rode one elephant through dense grass where rhinoceros' mothers roamed with babies. A mother with a baby charged at our elephant, creating pandemonium. The disturbance was soon quieted. We rode elephants at Amer Fort near Jaipur and the Coorg National Park in southern India.

I have been stung by a poisonous coral in the Great Barrier Reef near Cairns, North Eastern Australia while swimming underwater and watching the most colorful fish and coral. The sting was so powerful that it gave me a high fever and a hospital stay of a week while traveling with the 1989 International Bat Research Conference in Sydney, Australia.

Avoided dangerous waters

In Katora Taal, Gwalior, I was saved by my classmate Narayan. In Kila Sagar, my friend Rajjan, aka Mahendra Nath Saxena, saved me. The shallow river bed shifted suddenly at Sangam, Allahabad (confluence of Saraswati, Yamuna, and Ganga rivers). In the White River, Colorado, thrown out of the riverboat in a raging Class Five rapid. In Mexico, driving to a bat cave in Veracruz, a rain-swollen and shallow river, our vehicle stopped and restarted in both directions, midstream in the swelling river, with heavy rain continuing.

Other family members

A sketch drawn by Dr. KP Bhatnagar on May 15th 1961 in a letter written to his wife.

My grandfather was a scholar of Arabic, Persian, and Urdu-Hindi. My father was a statistician in Maharaja of Gwalior's secretariat. His boss was Virendra Sahai Saxena, who was not very kind to my father's loyal work. My father's terminal degree was a VIII (middle class) diploma from Janakganj Middle school. That was enough education to be a 'Babu' in those days. In the next generation, we had all sorts of education in our family: Kunwar (middle, high school, intermediate, B.Sc, M.Sc. Ph.D. (State Univ of New York at Buffalo, visiting professor Max Planck Institute for Brain Research, and many other honors), Raj Kumari Bhatnagar, my sister, BA, Ganesh MA (Hindi, principal of

115

a small high school who lost his life in a fatal bus accident he met while going for his daily travels to and from work every day. That day was fatal, for he said to his wife that he had no desire to go to work that day. But he did only pass away! Kailash MBBS, MD, Mahesh Asst Director Fisheries, Chanda veterinary surgeon, Kishan civil engineering.

In my family, Indu, BA, is a multi-talented wife, mother of two doctor daughters, four grandchildren, Alec Rouben, BA, the University of Colorado at Boulder, training as a YOGA MASTER at various schools of Yoga in Bangalore, India, then earning his MA degree in Yoga from the University of London, UK, and mother Divya, MD, and David Cantor, attorney. Cami Burruss, BA, MD, medicine, Bowman Gray Medical School, North Carolina, trained in Miniature Paintings, Chamba Style, under Padma Shree Vijay Sharma, Chamba, Himachal Pradesh, India, Clayton Burruss, University of Virginia, to be a medical professional with an MD, Matthew Burruss, computer sciences. Their father is a chemical engineer, David Burruss, and their mother, Jyoti, is a chemical engineer and an MD.

Indu's family has been detailed earlier. Indu's father, Brahma Shankar Varma (B.Sc Lahore University, Chemistry, peer published 1925-1974), and my brother-in-law Krishna Shankar Varma (Chemical Engineer, Chandigarh) specially trained in wax. Oils and establishment of factories in these specialties. Three sisters-in-law, Ravi & KIP Bhatnagar, running a high school in

Panchkula, Chandigarh, Shobha & Jagadish Bhatnagar, with son Ashish and Meeta Bhatnagar running the business of Chartered Accountant. The eldest of Indu's sisters, Shashi & JD Singh, a railway Police Officer, BS Varma, had a patent for making Camphor Cakes at Forest Res Inst, Dehradun. Indu with her parents traveled to Amarnath, a Hindu Temple in the Himalayas. Later after Divya's birth, I visited Indu, Vaishno Devi Temple, Kedarnath Temple, and Badrinath Temple. At Joshi Math, on the way to Badrinath, we had an audience with Swami Swarupananda, Shankaracharya for North East Indian maths. His darshan to our entire party was unique and still fresh in my mind. He was sitting on the wooden takhat surrounded by four ash-smeared Sadhus. Swami Ji conversed in English with us and had the knowledge of Kentucky on the world map. At another time, another Shankaracharya was traveling in Gwalior.

From the road, he noticed our Temple of Kaila Maharani and Kunwar Baba. He stopped there for his pujas and rested at the temple. I received the puja rice used and left it by him there upon my subsequent visit to India.

Gwalior Central Library

A sketch drawn by Dr. KP Bhatnagar in a letter written to his wife.

My lifeline for eight years. I was earning (a paltry sum) and educating myself and was greatly supported by the library staff. Starting with Shri Harishchandra, Shri Chandrika Prasad Mishra, and later Shri V S Moghe, both librarians in order, then Mr. Malhar Narayan Dharkar, my best friend, Makhan Lal Ojha, Narayan Prasad Mudgal, Ram Charan Lal Savita, Kallaji & Mangelal, the peons.

For years, I worked on the new book selection. I got to see and read new books to be purchased and other scholarly personalities such as Dr. Sri Ram Sharma (Professor of Political Science), Dr. Prakash Chandra (Principal and Professor of Political Science), and other high officials. I used to correspond when Dr. Sharma was in England for three years, receiving his blessings that I would someday be visiting abroad! It came true. After eight years of service at the library, it was difficult for me to separate. After some eight years of later serving as a college professor, I left for Buffalo, New York, in early 1967.

My CV should be consulted for the period 1967–current. While in the library, we picked Mr. Dhar. We (Dharkar, Ojha, Ramcharan, and Mudgal (he once said on these trips on Tuesdays, the library was closed) and I used to visit a new temple every Tuesday and engage in spiritual subjects. Mudgal once asked me if I would give him a seat in my car. At that time, I was a clerk alone and hardly owned a bicycle. The college I had to attend was at least 5 to 7 miles from the library. Mudgal was a Brahmin, and his blessings came true for me. Ganesh Vishnu Gore was another library assistant, a good friend of mine. Maheshwar Dayal Saxena joined the library as an assistant librarian, a mean man.

Spiritual matters discussed

A sketch drawn by Dr. KP Bhatnagar.

My family and I have been blessed by the Swamis: Swami Bhashyananda, President Maharaj of Belur Math Swami Ranganathananda, Swami Vibhudeshananda, all Ramakrishna Order Swamis visiting Louisville, Swami Dayananda, Swami Sumnananda (Mrs. Heera Sehra), Acharya Tahal Kishore Shastri (Kishore Bhai Vyas), and all dignitaries in this category. The beginning of this blessing came very early through my grandfather and father being devotees of Sri Kaila Maharani and Kunwar Baba, Gwalior. That is when I may have been 10–15 years old, of high school age. Our temple at Gwalior was some 5-7 miles away from home, and we, with our family, used to walk

120

that distance for all temple-related functions. My father will arrive directly from the office, which is close to Gwalior Railway Station, and my mother will bring his food from home, which she will eat after the midnight service.

At the age of 15, I was made the secretary of the Dev Samiti, Gwalior temple, by another senior member, Sri Gaya Prasad Srivastava. I had the support of all the members in every activity there. I think it was the year 1950. I moved away in July 1958. Our head Guru, Mahanta HeeraLal Maharaj, gave me a blessing that I have given so much in service of the temple that I will flourish in life to a great extent. Another time, during a Monday night prayer service, I suddenly began to cry out loudly. After a few minutes, my father put me at Maharaj's feet to receive his blessing, which he gave by saying "Sota Hai" (you sleep on the job). I was held by high fever and hallucinations for over a week with no explanation. Soon after this incident, we moved to Shivpuri; I was still hallucinating in high fever, locating tiny human beings playing their roles on the wall plaster. Even after some 50–60 years, those few weeks are very fresh in my mind. A few years back, I was visiting our temple. The Guruji was seated on His Gadi. He called me by motioning and said, "tell your fellow Samiti members that what they are observing is the same darshan. They will accept what you say."

I watched "Mere Sai: Shraddha Aur Saburi" (Sai Baba of Shirdi, near Nasik). I am finding great similarities between the actions of Sai Baba, on the one hand, and the Monday night service at the Gwalior temple prayer service, since at least 1925. The common observations between the two holy places are the presence of fire, the ongoing scenes in flames, and the capability of dealing with situations that ordinarily can be considered miracles (earlier, I had described our visit to a Sadhu who produced bananas,

sweets, and silver coins). The priest who established the Gwalior Temple in 1925 or earlier passed away in 1960; the Gaddi was not accessed by any Shaman (a word in the English Dictionary meaning a spiritual Guru capable of guiding spiritually). There is a news piece on a Shaman-Derek Shaman (a full page on him, Time Magazine, July 29, 2019, Shaman Finds His Queen), a sixth-generation Shaman in Berkeley, California. The spiritual prayer services seen at Gwalior, Sai Baba, and by Shamans (Webster's English Dictionary) at other centers share many similarities. Wherever miracle-like presentations are seen or shown, they are true, provided there is no outright fraud, which can be obvious, such as "card tricks" and others by the so-called magicians. El-Hifnawi was a post-doctoral research scholar from Egypt who came to Essen with a colleague of Prof. Manfred Bank's Black Scorpion, a 4-8-inch-long rock dwelling poison brought over from Egypt for research. In my presence, a white mouse was injected with the powdered poison. Within no time, the animal began to bleed from its nose and circled on its axis. Sorry for the animals.

My state of health 2019

A sketch drawn by Dr. KP Bhatnagar in a letter written to his wife.

Not good at all. For several years, the spinal stenosis has been becoming more painful with each passing day. Especially since Feb 6, 2019, a spinal stimulator has been implanted over my right pelvis. I take one 500mg Tylenol and one 25 mg tramadol at night to sleep. When I get up, it is with a' frozen' set of thigh muscles. I transfer to a leather chair and make several unsuccessful trips to the toilet after several maneuvers of taking painkillers. It takes me some half an hour to be fully operable. Jyoti and Divya have called to see how I'm doing.

Dr. Khairati Lal Gauri, our friend, passed away on Dec 16, 2019, after seriously going through painful experiences terminating in esophageal cancer, where he could not eat or even drink anything.

Yesterday, Indu and I celebrated New Year's Eve at Amar and Sudesh Singlas's (Dec 31, 2019). For the last several weeks, I have been very uncomfortable getting up in the morning.

Indu's help in keeping me safe is unbelievable. She is constantly doing all my responsibilities, taking care of doctor's appointments, medicines, telephones, Divya and Jyoti and their families, maintaining our house and numerous other functions, and driving. I have not driven since my spinal surgery (Feb 2019).

Today is May 27, 2020

Satyendra is not responding to my emails (four of them so far). The whole world is under the grip of COVID-19, the respiratory virus. I am saying a prayer every day for Satyendra. Today, the number of deaths in the USA from this virus is reported as 999883, soon expected to cross over 100,000 in this pandemic. My eyes are always wet, which makes me unable to see clearly.

The current status of our grandchildren is: Alec lives in Boulder, works for a health food company, and teaches yoga. Cami graduated with an MD (medicine), going to North Carolina from Wake Forest University in Child Psychiatry; Matthew graduated from Vanderbilt BA in Computer Sciences and a Masters in Computer Sciences; Clayton graduated in Chemical Engineering (University of Virginia) and has been admitted to the MD (medicine) program at the University of Kentucky, Lexington. His classes have begun. Cami has begun her residency in child psychiatry at the University of North Carolina at Chapel Hill.

Matthew has a job at Microsoft, and he is working from home in Louisville during this pandemic.

July 2, 2020

After being shut in Sri Lanka for two and a half months on Coronavirus issues, Krishna and Adu will fly to Bombay on May 29th. Which they did, quarantined in Mumbai and their homes in Jaipur. It is now, after an ordeal of nearly four months, that they are at home.

❄

List of items to be written but never completed

- Publications
- Honors and Awards
- Continents and Countries visited
- I am a Hindu – my understanding of the Hindu Philosophy – Sri Madbhagvad Gita, Sri MadBhagwat
- INDEX of Names and Events
- Names of classmates and teachers from various grades; recollections of graduate and Postgraduate faculty;
- Commissioned Offer in the Indian Army – NCC (National Cadet Corp)
- Sporadic writings – threads
- Indu- My Wife
- Sporadic writings
- Ramakrishna Vedanta

The Marriage of Science and Spice

Recipes
By
Indu Bhatnagar

Palak Paneer

Mint Chutney

Ingredients

1 bunch of mint leaves, cleaned
Raw mango skin, sliced
1-3 green chili peppers
Fresh coriander leaves (If mint is not enough)
3-4 garlic cloves
1 tsp salt
Lemon juice
Jaggary (Gur)

Instructions

Place all items in blender and add salt, lemon juice, and brown sugar to the paste.
Place in glass jar.
Keep in refrigerator.

Lemon Pickle

Ingredients

6 lemons
3 tbsp salt
1-2 tbsp cayenne pepper

Instructions

Wash the lemons well.
Cut in quarters and remove all seeds.
Add the lemons, salt and pepper to blender.
Blend until chopped well. Store in glass jar with secure lid
and place in sun for 2-3 days.
Then keep in fridge.

Upma

Mango Pickle

Ingredients

Unripe mango
Mustard oil (olive oil is a good substitute)
Mango masala mixture (Swad brand is best)
1 tsp Salt (or to taste)
¼ tsp Asafoetida (Hing)

Instructions

Cut mango (including the pit if available) into chunky pieces.
Heat oil, then allow it to cool.
Add mango, hing, mango masala mixture, and salt.
Keep it in a glass jar at room temperature to marinate several days before serving.

Roti

Ingredients

2 cups whole wheat flour
Warm water
1 tbsp cooking oil

Instructions

Mix above to make a stiff dough.
Knead until smooth and elastic.
Let it sit for 30 minutes.
Roll into 2-inch balls.
Dredge in dry flour to roll it out as thin as possible.
Cook on a griddle (Tawa) on medium heat. Cook on the flip side too.
Press lightly with a towel on the edges until it swells.
Melt some butter on the cooked roti before serving to soften it.

Puris

Similar to rotis for the ingredients, add some oil and dredge in a small amount to roll out the ball. Fry in hot oil. Let it fluff on one side before flipping to the other side. Press the edges with the spatula to help it rise. Drain on a paper towel before serving.

Paratha
Recipe on page 140

Bhatura

Ingredients

2 cups bleached all-purpose flour
1 packet active dry yeast
½ tsp salt
1/3 to ½ cup water
Oil for deep frying

Instructions

Dissolve yeast in warm water and let it sit for 10 minutes. Make dough with flour, water/yeast, and salt. Leave in a warm place for 6 hours, periodically kneading it. Make small balls and roll them out like puri and deep fry. Serve sizzling.

Paratha

Ingredients

1-2 cups whole wheat flour
Finely diced vegetables or cooked potatoes

Instructions

Make the dough as made for the Roti. Once it is rolled out, grease one side and add the vegetables. Then place another rolled-out dough on top of it and pinch the edges together to seal it. Add a little melted butter along the edges to help it seal the edges. Roll this stuffed paratha out, so the vegetables stick inside. Cook on the hot griddle as the Roti. Add melted butter.

Sabudana (Sago) Khichdi

Stuffed Okra

Ingredients

1pound fresh okra, cut partially lengthwise
2 tbsp gram flour
1tsp cumin powder
1 tbsp coriander powder
1 tsp amchur (mango mixture; buy from Indian grocery store)
2 tbsp of cooking oil
½ tsp red chili powder
1 tsp salt
2 tbsp cooking oil

Instructions

Heat oil in frying pain.
Roast gram flour until it turns golden.
Transfer it to a bowl. Add spices.
Fill okra with this mixture.
In the same pan, add oil and the okra cook on medium heat for about 10-15 minutes, and cover the dish.
Do not add water.

Okra

Ingredients

Cut 3 large handfuls of okra
in bite size pieces (don't
place in water)
3 tbsp cooking oil
1tbsp Ajwain spice
3 tbsp crushed peanuts
(optional)
½ tsp cayenne pepper
1 tbsp turmeric
2 tbsp coriander powder
1 tsp fennel seeds
1 tsp amchur (mango mixture; buy from Indian grocery
store)
Fresh lemon

Instructions

Use a flat pan for cooking.
Heat oil.
Add ajwain and roast it.
Add the cut okra, and squeeze some lemon juice over the
okra.
Add the rest of the pepper, salt to taste, turmeric, cayenne
pepper, coriander powder, and fennel seed.
Once it is cooked, then add crushed peanuts and amchur.

Kalonji (Spicy Cooked Mango)

Ingredients

2 tbsp. Kalonji (black seeds like onion seeds)
Unripe mango, remove the skin, cut in chunky pieces and
cut the pit if able
1 tsp Asafoetida (Hing)
Salt to taste
1 tsp cayenne pepper to taste
1 tbsp turmeric
Brown sugar to taste
1-2 tbsp cooking oil

Instructions

Heat the oil.
Add Asafoetida and Kalonji.
Add salt, pepper, and turmeric.
Cook this, and then add Mango.
Add water to fill the top of the Mango.
Once the Mango is soft, and the water is boiling, add some
jaggery to taste.

Kulfi (Indian ice cream)

Ingredients

Fat free sweetened condensed milk
Low fat evaporated milk
Low fat Cool Whip
Pistachios (crushed)

Instructions

Combine all ingredients, place in Popsicle sticks, and
freeze until ready to serve.
Add other flavors, i.e., mango bits or other fruits as desired.

Cauliflower Sabzi

Cauliflower Sabzi

Ingredients

Cut small pieces of cauliflower
Carrots, peas, broccoli, potatoes can also be added (add
more spices)
1-2 tbsp cooking oil
1 tbsp cumin seeds
1 tbsp chopped ginger
½ tsp paprika
1 tbsp coriander powder
½ tsp turmeric
1 tbsp garam masala
½ tsp red chili powder
Salt to taste
Fresh coriander leaves
chopped
Amchur powder to taste

Instructions

Heat the oil in a pan.
Add cumin seeds and roast.
Add ginger and gently cook.
Add vegetables, then the other spices, and cook over
medium heat for 15-20 minutes till cauliflower is tender.
When almost cooked, add Amchur, and garam masala to
taste. Then serve with coriander leaves sprinkled on top.

Dahl (lentils)

Ingredients

1 cup dahl- soak one hour in water before cooking
1 tsp Asafoetida
2 tbsp Cumin seeds
4 Garlic cloves crushed
1-2 Bay leaf
1 cinnamon stick
1 tsp Cayenne pepper
Salt to taste
Turmeric
2-4 Black pepper (whole)
1-2 Clove (whole)
2-3 small tomatoes (diced)

Instructions

In a pot, heat some oil.
Add Asafoetida and cumin seeds.
Then add garlic, with the rest of the spices and tomatoes.
Mix and cook till tomatoes are soft.
Add dahl and then 3 cups of water.
Cook till water is boiling and dahl is cooked.
Also, make this in a slow cooker by adding all the
ingredients and keeping low heat.

Poha (Puffed rice)

Ingredients

1-2 tbsp cooking oil
1 medium size onion diced
2 cups dried poha, add water to
fully moisten and then squeeze
out remaining water
1 tbsp cumin seeds
Salt to taste
Cayenne pepper to taste
1 tbsp turmeric
1 boiled potatoes (peeled and
diced)
Peas
Cauliflower pieces
Coriander chopped
Lemon juice to taste

Instructions

In a separate bowl, add the salt, pepper, and turmeric to the
wet poha and set aside.
Heat oil, add onion, and roast lightly.
Add potatoes, peas, and cauliflower, if available.
Roast the vegetables in the oil.
Add poha with spices and a dash of sugar.
Cook and stir over low heat for several minutes.
Squeeze fresh lemon juice and add coriander leaves for
garnishment before serving.
2 cups of dry poha will serve 2-3 people

Kadhi

Pakori (Fritters) for Besan Curry

Ingredients

2-3 cups Besan (aka gram flour/chick pea flour)
1/2 tsp hing

Instructions

Add hing to dry besan.
Add enough water to make a mix that is thick like pancake batter. *Use an electric mixer to make it fluffy.*
It will be mixed enough when a small amount floats in the water.
Heat oil for frying. Pour (or use your fingers) to drop a small ball into the hot oil. Fry till done; 4-6 minutes. Then, place in cool water. Squeeze the water gently out of the pakori, being careful to not break the ball.

Chickpea fritters in Curry (Besan Curry)

Ingredients

Heat 3 tbsp cooking oil in wok
2 tbsp Cumin seeds
½ tsp Hing
1 tbsp Mustard seeds
1 tbsp Fenugreek seeds (Methi)
2 tbsp Turmeric
Salt to taste
Cayenne Pepper to taste
1 cup Besan (chick pea flour or gram flour)
3 cups plain yogurt

Instructions

Mix besan with yogurt.
It should be very thin in consistency. Heat the oil in a wok.
Add hing and the seeds to the hot oil and cook till the seeds start popping.
Add the turmeric, salt, and pepper to the yogurt/besan mix.
Then, add this yogurt/besan mixture to the oil.
Cook on low heat for 20-30 minutes, stirring frequently and constantly, so it does not stick to the bottom. Once cooked, add the cooked/cooled to the mixture. The older the yogurt, it will be sourer and help this dish taste better.

Squash (Kadu)

Ingredients

Squash (ripe squash has hard skin and the skin will need to be cut off; unripe squash has soft skin and this can be cooked). Soak in water to help it soften for 10-15 minutes.
Cooking oil
¼ tsp Hing
2-3 tbsp Fenugreek seeds (Methi)
2 tbsp Tumeric
Salt
Cayenne Pepper

Instructions

Heat the oil, add hing and then add methi seeds to cook gently.
Add the squash.
Add turmeric, salt, and pepper.
Cover and allow to cook gently over 15-20 minutes over medium heat.

Chicken Curry

Chicken Curry

Ingredients

3 lbs. Chicken that is cleaned well and as much of the fat removed 6 pieces
Yogurt
Ginger (4 inch long)
Garlic (3 cloves)
2 onions
¼ tsp Hing
2 tbsp Cumin seeds
3 whole cloves
2-3 whole Black pepper
1 bay leaf
2 tbsp Turmeric
2 tbsp Coriander powder
1 whole Cardamom
1-2 tbsp Curry powder masala mix
Cayenne pepper
Salt
Fresh tomatoes (or tomato puree can)
Chopped fresh coriander leaves
Garam masala

Instructions

Soak the chicken in yogurt as long as you have time.
Grind the ginger and garlic and set aside.
Grind the onions and tomatoes and set them aside.

Heat some cooking oil in a pressure cooker or a regular stock pot.

Add hing and let this roast.

Add ground onion and cook the onion gently.

Add the cumin seeds and cook some more. Now add the ginger/garlic, salt, turmeric, cloves, bay leaf, ground coriander, whole cardamom, curry powder mix, and cayenne pepper.

Let these spices cook together.

Next, add the chicken and cook for 15-20 minutes over medium heat.

Add the tomatoes and cook for a few minutes.

Now add enough water to cover the chicken.

If placed under pressure, cook for 3 whistles under medium heat.

If in a stock pot, cook on medium heat for 20 minutes.

Once it is cooked, add garam masala to taste and garnish with fresh coriander.

It is also possible to add chat masala if it needs to be tangier.

Eggplant Sabzi

Ingredients

1 whole eggplant cut in ¾" thick circular slices
1 tsp cumin powder
½ tsp turmeric
2 tbsp coriander powder
1 tsp red pepper
1 tsp salt
1 tsp amchur (dried mango powder)
½ cup cooking oil

Instructions

Mix all the spices together. Heat oil in a frying pan, and then add the eggplant.
Sprinkle the spices on each side and fry till done.

Sambar

Ingredients

1 cup Urad dahl lentil (no skin)
Salt
1-2 tbsp sambar masala mix
½ tsp turmeric
fresh coriander chopped

Instructions

Soak dahl for 30-60 min till it is soft.
The longer the soaking time, the less cooking time.
Make sure the dry dahl does not have any oil.
Oil in the storage process makes the final dish taste poorly.
Pour the softened dahl with water in the pressure cooker, and add salt.
Place a metal bowl with any vegetables on hand into the pressure cooker with the dahl with some water.
Vegetables include pearl onion, squash, okra, eggplant, radish, and peeled potato.
Cook on high heat for 2 whistles.
Once you can open the pressure cooker, pour the vegetables into the dahl. Add the sambar masala and turmeric, along with freshly chopped coriander. Cook on low heat for 20-30 minutes.
Before serving, make some Tarka by heating some oil or ghee; add dried red pepper, curry leaves, 1 tsp mustard seeds, and 2 tsp paprika. Pour 1/2 tsp on each bowl before serving. Serve with Idly or Dosa.
Use GITS Rava Idly mix.

Saag

Ingredients

1 kg finely chopped mustard green (sarso)
¼ finely chopped
spinach
2 red chilies
½ tsp minced ginger
4 cloves garlic (minced)
2 tbsp gram flour
1 tbsp butter
2 green chilies (minced)
Ghee or 4 tbsp cooking
oil
Salt per taste

Instructions

Boil the mustard and spinach leaves till soft.
If using fresh leaves, wash very well.
Can use frozen.
Set aside in another pan. In the pot, heat the ghee/oil.
Add green chilies, garlic, ginger, and broken red chilies.
Sauté the spices till they brown. Add the cooked
mustard/spinach to the water.
Mix the above with an emulsion blender.
Mix the gram flour with a little water to make a paste.
Add this to the dish. Cook for about 20-30 minutes on low
heat.
Serve with tarka or a pat of butter. Add paneer if you like
(buy from the Indian grocery store).

Chole (Chickpea Curry)

Ingredients

2 cups dry chickpea
2 tbsp oil
1 onion, finely chopped
1 bay leaf
2 tsp minced garlic, ginger
2 tomatoes, chopped
2 tsp coriander powder and amchur (dried mango powder)
2 tsp roasted cumin powder
salt to taste
1 tsp garam masala and paprika
2 tsp turmeric
½ tsp black pepper
cayenne pepper to taste
1 whole cardamom
Fresh cilantro, chopped

Instructions

Soak the chickpeas overnight (the longer, the better, as it helps with the digestion of legumes).
Drain, rinse and set aside.
Heat oil, add onions, and cook till starting to brown.
Add all other spices and then the tomatoes.
Cook over medium heat for 5-7 minutes. Add chickpeas and water.
Cook in a pressure cooker for 2-3 whistles or in a regular pot, stirring for 30-40 minutes.
Garnish with cilantro.

Pani Puri (Gol Gappa)

Package of masala of Pani Puri.
Dried mint leaves.
Fresh lemon juice.
Gol Gappa premade (purchase at an Indian store).
Mix the package with mint leaves and fresh lemon juice.
Serve with canned chickpeas, diced boiled potatoes,
tamarind chutney, and mint chutney.

Bittergourd (Kerala)

Ingredients

Fresh Bitter gourd (can use frozen) as much as you want to make
1 large diced Onion
1 tbsp. Cumin
1 tbsp. Amchur
1 tbsp. Fennel seed
2 tbsp. Ground Coriander
1 tbsp. Cayenne pepper (to taste)
2 tbsp. Turmeric
1 tbsp. Methi seeds (fenugreek)
Salt to taste

Instructions

For fresh bitter gourd, lightly scrape the surface and soak in salt water overnight.
This will help reduce the bitterness of the vegetable.
If using frozen bitter gourd, then this step is not necessary.
When ready to prepare, decide whether you want to make stuffed or just cut pieces in circles.
The stuffing is the same masala for the bitter gourd cut in circles.
If stuffing the bitter gourd, slice lengthwise without slicing through.

Add the diced onions in a bit of hot oil till softened. Set aside.

Add more oil, heat up, add all other spices and allow to cook till fragrant. Add the onions.

Stuff into the bitter gourd and tie the white cotton thread to hold it together.

In the same pot, add some oil, heat this oil and slowly cook the bitter gourd, turning carefully.

If cooking, the circle shape can add fresh carrots and potatoes you have on hand to the masala mixture. Then add the circle shape bitter gourd and slowly cook over low heat till done.

❄

The Marriage of Science and Spice

Made in the USA
Middletown, DE
31 August 2022

72850117R00091